Watc

Watching Over Rains

By

T. J. Howard

JoNa Books
Bedford, Indiana

ISBN: 1932673016

LCCN: 2003113132

First printing November 2003

Watching Over Rains

The Story of Cecil Rains

with T.J. Howard

~ Dedication ~

To the brave American men and women who have answered their country's call to duty in defense of freedom

Introduction

I have always been fascinated by the study of World War II. Over the years this has included delving into many books, watching hours of video documentaries, and even interviewing men who were actual participants in the "big one".

No Hollywood producer could have matched the actual script played out during the unfolding of World War II. The magnitude of the cast of characters who played lead roles was absolutely astounding. Just the mention of names like Roosevelt, Truman, Churchill, Hitler, Stalin, Mussolini, and Hirohito evoke the bold presence they displayed as they led their respective countries during the political and military campaigns.

You had the "bad guys" riding into town clearly wearing their "black hats" represented by the brutality of trampling many innocent victims throughout Europe during their quest for world domination. You had the "good guys" appear on the scene clearly wearing "white hats" represented by their devotion to defend the weak, uphold the rights of the oppressed, and protect their cherished way of life. Then there were the Soviets who seemed to be the only participant in a hat of somewhat of a gray tint. It was definitely a filmmaker's dream, but this war was no dream. Unfortunately, it was very real.

It's difficult to imagine that one could ever overstate the implications that resounded from the outcome of World War II. The entire implemented world governmental structure was seemingly up for grabs. The American way of life was being threatened. Almost to a man, the entire country sprang to action after the devastating surprise attack on our naval base at Pearl Harbor. The individual implications created by the outbreak of war were then filtered down to the American family. The stories of the sacrifices made by the families represented by the millions of participants are endless.

The resounding effect of World War II has always been very evident in my family. My father, Warren G. Howard answered his country's call to duty. He had been an extremely talented athlete throughout his youth. He was much renowned throughout the area for his strong pitching arm. He had a tryout opportunity with the Chicago Cubs, but decided to join the army instead of attending. The Cubs could wait. He had what he considered a more important matter to attend to, his service to his country. He could always go to the tryout when he returned, at least that's what he thought at the time. He would never get that chance.

My father was stationed in the Southwest Pacific. While there, he contracted malaria and almost died. When he recovered enough to return to active duty, he was severely hit by shrapnel in both legs. He barely survived the injury and after an extended recovery period eventually made it back to his Southern Illinois home. This tragic turn of events ended any thoughts of a possible baseball career. He was disabled and continued in poor health until his death in 1967. It's impossible to even approach the enormous impact my father's service in World War II had on his life and the life of our entire family.

Even though there were incredibly negative ramifications from his service, I'm sure that given the chance my father would have done the same thing again in a heartbeat. My family was just one of many who was impacted by the sacrifice of family members who wanted to serve their country.

I always enjoyed listening to the accounts of the war relayed to me by my late father in law, Durward L. Book and also many other men of that generation that served in World War II. I'm sure there are an unfathomable number of similar stories out there, some with many more heartbreaking circumstances. After all, though he was severely injured and his dream of a baseball career was gone, my father did return home, unlike many others who served.

When I began work on this book, Cecil Rains and I both lived in Bonnie, Illinois, a small town in the Southern part of the state. I first heard the story of his exploits during World War II when he made an appearance at Ina Grade School, the small elementary school in which I taught. He was absolutely amazing. One of the things that you try to do as a teacher is to try to make significant events from history more than just material from textbooks. It makes the study of history much more meaningful to students. Cecil's presentation did just that concerning our study of World War II.

Cecil would be the first to tell you that his story was not that much unlike many others, but it is an inspiring story that definitely deserves to be told. I hope you as a reader enjoy reading about Cecil's life as much as I have enjoyed hearing about it and putting it down on paper.

T.J. Howard

Chapter 1

What in the world were they thinking?

That's the question I found going through my mind as I watched the pondering faces of these young American teens as they made their way across the English Channel on their way toward what would be the largest one-day invasion in world history.

What should a man (I use the term very loosely since I was sixteen years old at the time.) be thinking as he faces such an obstacle? Even though many of us were barely out of puberty, we were not ignorant of what we were about to face. Our commanding officers had been very frank with us about the impending operation.

The Germans were entrenched in France and were well prepared to defend any attempt at liberation by the Allies. We also surmised that they would be on the alert since they knew we were coming at some point. Our only hope of surprise could come by when and where the invasion would occur.

Our superiors had hoped that the time would be somewhat of a surprise, but in reality we knew the German forces were most likely expecting an attempted invasion at any moment. It was doubtful we could catch them off guard. Our greatest chance at surprise came from the location of our strike. The word had filtered down that the Germans would likely expect an invasion from a location in the north. For this reason our braintrusts had chosen Normandy, which was south of what would have been the most expected location of an operation, as our target. Even if, in fact, our strategy was effective, each of us realized that casualties would be incredibly high. We knew there was a great likelihood that we would not see tomorrow.

I found myself gazing into the eyes of each individual soldier. What was their story? Did they have a family back home waiting for them? Were they going to make it home to them? Were they even going to make it through the day? Were they scared? Were they thinking what I was thinking?

That last question was the most difficult to answer because even I didn't know what I was thinking as our craft made it's way closer and closer to the beaches of Normandy, France on that day in the wee hours of June 6, 1944. I knew my young life might be at its end. They say when a person has a near death experience that their life flashes before their eyes. I found myself thinking about my life up to that point. There was definitely a lot of life to think about.

I was born in Makanda, Illinois in February of 1926. Makanda is a small town in the southern part of the state of Illinois. My birthday is officially listed as February 3, 1926, but the actual exact day of my birth is questionable. You see I was not born under what would be considered "normal" circumstances in the twenties. I was born to my mother, Evelyn Hayes, who was not married at the time.

In today's somewhat more liberal society this unfortunately has become rather commonplace, but it was something that was almost unheard of in 1926. It was just about taboo to even speak the word "pregnant" let alone find yourself in that condition. Premarital pregnancies did happen back then, though I guess not at the alarming rate of today, but the reaction to them by society was startlingly different.

Families sometimes went to great lengths to avoid the stigma and shame of out of wedlock pregnancies. Many times the girl who found herself expecting would be sent away to stay with family out of town until she delivered her baby. Sometimes the baby might be given up for adoption, might be given to another family member to raise, or in some instances the woman would keep the baby and try to deal with the stares and finger pointing as she raised the youngster. This was definitely not an easy set of circumstances to deal with for mother or child.

If the woman did decide to keep her baby it made it very difficult for her entire family. In many instances girls were told to stay away from the family, almost being disowned because of the reproach that would be thought to have been brought to the family's good name. It doesn't seem very compassionate or understanding and I can't imagine doing this to your own daughter no matter what you thought of her behavior, but it was done none the less.

I guess the best case scenario for an unwed mother facing bringing a child into the world on her own was for the father of the child to decide to marry her and as they say "give the child a name". It was considered the respectable thing to do for the father to "make an honest woman" of the young mother to be by proposing marriage. Even though it was the preferable alternative, it was not the way it worked out for my mother and me.

My biological father, I learned many years later, was a young man who was at the time from Makanda. I don't know a lot about the details of the relationship between the two of them since my mother would never talk about it. I don't know how serious the two were about each other. My guess is that as happens sometimes with teens, they just let things progress a little too far, too soon. It's all speculation though on my part.

For whatever reason my parents never got married. I heard that my father left the area. If stories I heard were true, he may not have fled as much to avoid his responsibility to my mother as much as to save his life. I always heard tell that my grandfather, Moses Hayes, my mother's father, went after my biological father with a twelve gauge shot gun after hearing of the situation. Knowing my grandfather, I don't have a difficult time believing this at all. Because of this and the simple fact that he and my mother were so very young at the time, I have never had any bitter feelings toward my father. I know this might be difficult for some to believe, but it's true. It's just my nature I guess to forgive and not hold grudges. It's a trait of mine that has come in very handy in many situations over the years.

I never got the opportunity to meet my biological father. I was told that he moved to Colorado, married, and had a family. I also heard that several years later he returned to Southern Illinois where he remained until his death.

Over the years I have often wondered about my father, what it would have been like to have met him. I also have thought a lot about the relatives I have somewhere, who probably know nothing about my existence. With all the interest in family trees and with the internet as a great tool as of late, I've contemplated trying to track some of them down. It would be interesting to meet them and discuss the type of man my father turned out to be. I have never been one to dwell on these things, but I would welcome the opportunity to question them about my dad. Do I look like him, or share some of his personality characteristics? I would be interested to know the answers to these and other questions I would have.

My mother decided to keep me and raise me at home with the help of her parents, my grandparents, Moses and May Hayes. My mother had three brothers and a sister, so there wasn't much room in the small home and money was very tight with eight mouths to feed.

A few months after I was born my grandfather got a job at a mine in Pittsburg, Illinois, which is a very small town about seven miles east of Marion. It was too far to commute from Makanda, so grandfather moved us over to Pittsburg. We lived in a one-bedroom home near the mine. I can remember spending many a night sharing a mattress placed on the floor with my aunt and uncles.

Not long after we moved to Pittsburg my life would make another change as my mother met and married a man by the name of Audie Rains. He was a World War I veteran who was a bootlegger during prohibition and drank his creations on a much too regular basis. We moved out of my grandparents home and into another extremely small abode. Although, Audie Rains did not officially adopt me, I took his last name. I called him dad and for the first several years of my life I believed that he was in fact my father. I knew from my very earliest recollections that there was a definite edge to the relationship between my dad and me. As an innocent youngster, I couldn't understand why, but I never got a feeling of closeness from him.

Over the next few years my parents had four more children all approximately two years apart. First there were my brothers, Henry and then Audie Ray. Then came my sister, Bette Jean and finally my brother, Jackie Dee. After my siblings' births, the fact that there was something different about me became more and more evident.

As desperately as I tried I just never seemed to be able to do anything to suit my dad. I walked on pins and needles around him, but I always seemed to do something to upset him. At the time I thought it was my fault, that I was the one who couldn't seem to measure up. Over the years I finally came to understand that my father just never accepted the fact that I was not his biological son and that my mother had been with another man. There was nothing I could do to change that, but my stepfather sure made me pay a huge price for this fact through the years.

I was given a very burdensome load of chores to do almost from the time I could walk. It was a regimen that would probably land a parent in jail today. One of my jobs included bringing in the coal. This may sound harmless enough, but it was more than walking outside and carrying in a few chunks of the solid heating fuel. I had to walk about a quarter of a mile to get to an old strip mine in the area. I had to unearth the coal needed to fill my pull wagon, though I could barely even carry the shovel let alone do the very laborious digging involved. I then had to manage to drag home the wagon full of coal to heat our home.

We also burned wood to provide heat in our small shack. You can probably guess whose job it was to cut the wood. There were no chain saws back then either. I would have been too young to operate one even if there were. I was also too young to swing the ax I used, but that didn't seem to matter. I had to cut the wood, split it, and bring it in. I sometimes look at young children today that are probably about the age I was at the time I dug the coal and chopped the wood for our family and shudder at the thought of them having to do that kind of work at that age. Don't get me wrong, I believe that kids would benefit from a fair amount of chores and responsibility, but not even close to the situation that I found myself in. Another point I want to make clear is that many kids in the twenties and thirties had to do their share and maybe more of work to help their families, but to my knowledge not usually to the extent of mine.

When I had reached school age I was allowed to attend school three days a week. That's right, I said allowed. I know that would be a novel idea to most kids today that would rather be allowed to stay home than be forced to go to school. They would prefer their home where they could play, watch television, and such. I knew what I would be doing if I stayed home – work, and that's just what I did.

On the other two days of the week in which I wasn't allowed to go to school I would help my mother wash and iron the family's clothes. Again, you have to remember that this was before the days of the household washer and drying and the electric irons. As people who lived during this time can probably recall, washing and ironing in those days was a very laborious task.

I would carry the bundles of clothes down to the creek where my mother and I would fill tubs with water. We would scrub the clothing with soap until clean and then dip the clothes into a rinse. We then would ring the clothes out by hand, which was a difficult task especially for the heavy denim type overalls and such. It makes my hands hurt just to think about it. We would then take the clean bundle back to hang to dry.

When the clothes were dry enough to iron we would begin this burdensome task. We would use one of two irons that we would set on the stove to warm. We would use one of the irons until it was too cool to be effective and then put it back on the stove to warm while taking the other, now warm one. We would continue this practice of trading irons back and forth until all the clothes were pressed. It usually took us one full day to do the washing and one full day to do the ironing. I had to help my mother get these jobs done while still doing my regular chores. It was definitely a full days work. It still makes me tired today just to think about it.

On those wash days it really seemed to hit home to me how I was definitely treated differently as I watched my siblings that were old enough walk out of the door to attend school. I had always reasoned that I was forced to work so hard because I was the oldest child, but eventually came to realize that there was much more to it than that. I had just assumed that when they were old enough that my sister and brothers would take on some of my responsibilities. As far as I know, they never did.

I don't mean to paint a picture that presents the impression that my siblings had a life of luxury. They had a difficult time also. It was the depression era and things were very tough for our whole family. We had almost no money and really had very little to eat. I can remember going to bed many a night still hungry and my sister and brothers sometimes felt the same way I'm sure.

I'm also sure many people who had to live through the late twenties and the thirties can relate to the fact that I was forced to work so hard at such a young age. Almost all of the kids I knew at that time did things to help the family make it through. Some of the kids helped on the farm, or around the house. I even knew kids who had paying jobs and used the money to help the family have enough to eat. Even though work for someone my age wasn't that uncommon in our area in the thirties, I didn't know any child my age that had anywhere near the burdensome load that I had.

Still, to this day, I can honestly say that the work itself didn't bother me. I really felt a sense of satisfaction and a great sense of accomplishment at doing things to help my mother and the family. I didn't even mind the hunger I had sometimes – the hunger for food that is. It was the other hunger that was devastating – the hunger for love.

In all the many times I did my chores and helped out around the house, which included sacrificing my school studies at least two full days a week, I never remember my parents making one positive comment about my accomplishments. I never once remember them saying "Thanks for your help." or "Good job, son." I don't even remember a simple pat on the back and a smile – not once. This was what really hurt, not the calluses, the sore muscles, the cuts and bruises that I sometimes incurred while performing my daily duties. What really hurt me was the complete and total lack of affection by my parents.

While I didn't completely understand all the reasons why at the time, I soon came to realize, if not accept, that for some reason my father did not seem to love me like he did the rest of the children.

What in the world is a "bastard"? That's what I tried to figure out for many years. I heard my father use the term many times during their arguments. I didn't know the meaning of the term, but it didn't take me long to realize that whatever it meant it was definitely not good.

As I got a little older and eventually realized the meaning of the term, "bastard", I picked up on the rest of the story line of the argument. My father would bring up my mother's past. He would talk about her younger days before they were married, about her apparent promiscuous behavior, at least in his opinion. He seemed to be paranoid that she would revert back to the same lifestyle. He was always accusing her of being unfaithful to him. Even though she vehemently denied the charge he continued relentlessly until he eventually got around to mentioning her "bastard".

Amazingly enough my father was basically a pretty likeable guy to the average person who would meet him. He seemed to treat people, with the exception of me, very well. He could be very pleasant and kind in his everyday dealings. It seemed that most people in our area were actually very fond of him, when he wasn't drinking. The problem was, he was almost always drinking.

Having my father in charge of owning and operating a still was in my opinion kind of like putting the mouse in charge of the cheese, as they say. It was a pretty easy leap to make, I guess. He used the alcohol to make a living. He had to make a large amount of it to distribute. Because of this he was constantly trying it out himself. He had to make sure it was acceptable to his customers so they'd be back. He knew that all it would take would be one bad batch to steer potential customers away. When word got out of this his business would be ruined. It would just be natural for a person to develop a taste for the stuff and my father sure did.

I used to watch my father as he sat around drinking and wonder why a man would want to do this. I learned to despise the smell of the stuff, as my father would reek of alcohol as he came in after drinking. I sometimes felt sorry for myself in my situation, but I felt even more sorry for my mother. The person I found myself feeling most sorry for, as hard as it may be to believe, was my father.

During this time period jobs were very hard to find. Most all of the usual places in the Southern Illinois area that had always done their share of hiring were not only not taking on anyone, they were usually laying people off because of the severe depression gripping the country. My father had not found any work and was using his bootlegging business to support his family, or at least try to support us. If he did at one time pursue some other employment, he probably became discouraged and eventually gave up trying. It would be many years later before he would have an actual job away from home. I'm sure that this was very disheartening, as it would be to any man trying to take care of his family. It would probably make any man feel like he had let the people in his life who were depending on him down, that he was a failure.

My father may have used alcohol to forget his troubles as many people with problems do. Many people do this, but my father had too easy access to the stuff to resist it if it served as some type of relief from the worries of life he was facing. He fell into a vicious cycle that many people do when facing a problem with alcohol. He was probably depressed by his situation in life, then used the alcohol to forget, to seemingly get away from his troubles. The problem was that when he sobered up the problems he faced with the finances, and dealing with me my mother's past were still there. He never really actually seemed to face the problems. As most people who use alcohol as an escape realize, all you add to your problems is one more problem, an alcohol problem. My father sure developed one. It was sad. Even though he treated me so harshly, I sure felt sorry for him.

Chapter 2

Grandparents are usually very important in the lives of their grandchildren. They are many times able to provide a support system in the nurturing of a youngster. (If mom and dad say no, ask grandma and grandpa.) Years ago it seems to me that the average child may have been closer to his or her grandparents. This happened back then because in many situations in that day and age several generations of family members lived under the same roof. Families were sometimes forced into this situation for economic reasons. I guess it's nice for kids today it seems that most, though not all, families are able to afford to give their offspring more than they had themselves. Because of this fact, I think we've grown farther apart from these important family relationships.

The only person during my childhood that showed me any affection was my grandfather, Moses Hayes. I guess we developed this close bond because I had no father at home when I was born and grandpa filled that role for me.

Since I was so very young when my mother married Audie Rains, he had the opportunity to fill the gap left by the absence of my real father. Had he given me the love and support that most fathers provide for their children, I honestly believe that I would have had the same love for him that I would've felt had he been my actual father. I say this very confidently because for the first several years of my life I believed he was my father. If he had shown me any affection, I would have thought the world of him – but he didn't.

The only person who did show his love for me was quite a character. That's why as I said earlier that it wasn't hard for me to believe that he took out after my real father when he heard I was on the way. He fascinated me. I loved to just watch him go about his routines around his house. The way that most kids watch their dads, I watched him. If he did something, then I wanted to do it because if grandpa did it then I thought it must be the right thing to do because he knew everything, at least that's what I believed at the time.

I loved to go places with him. He used to take me with him when he would go into town and such. I actually felt like he was proud to have me with him which was something I never felt with my parents. If grandpa had any money at the time, he would buy me candy and sometimes even a toy. He seemed to love to buy these things for me as much as I loved getting them. He sure made me feel special.

If my parents had let me I would have moved in with my grandparents. I always thought that my parents probably would have preferred this if it were not for the fact that they wouldn't have me around to relieve them of the chores that I performed. I thought about telling them that I would continue to do the chores if they would have just let me stay with grandpa, but I never got the nerve to ask my father. I was too scared of how he might react. I'm sure he wouldn't have agreed to it, anyway.

Looking back now, it appeared that my father and grandfather had a very strained relationship at best. On one hand, I believe that my grandfather was fond of my dad. After all, as I said earlier most people thought my father was a very good man and in many ways he was. I know, like most other people in town, that my grandfather respected the fact that Audie Rains was a veteran of World War I. At that time veterans were treated with the utmost respect.

I don't want to give the impression that no one gives veterans their due respect today, because I believe that most people do. I have been very fortunate in this aspect. Almost all of the people that I have encountered in my treks to tell my story have given me the warmest of welcomes and have treated with the utmost respect. This includes people from U.S. Congressmen to elementary school children. I am in no way bitter about any mistreatment on my part, but I have heard many stories of veterans that have not been so fortunate. As a country we still have a ways to go in this area, but I personally have no complaints.

I also believe that my grandfather had a great amount of respect for my father because he took in his daughter, who was an unwed mother at the time. This was more of an oddity than it is today. Audie had married his daughter and given me his name. I'm sure that my grandfather along with most of the other people around town respected Audie for this also.

I never remember my grandfather making mention of this issue. I do remember him asking questions of me especially when we were alone on one of our outings to town. I didn't realize it then, but I'm sure he was pumping me for information about what went on when he wasn't around. I can remember some looks of disgust as he thought about the circumstances that we were going through, though he never actually mentioned the issue openly, at least to me. He may have discussed it with my mother, but I'm not aware of it.

Since I never talked to grandpa about the issue, I'm not sure of his thoughts, but there were definitely some reasons that my grandpa would have stayed out of it. As I talked about earlier, it was unusual for a man to decide to take in a woman who already had a child in tow. My grandpa may have believed that even though things weren't exactly perfect, it would be even worse if my mother left Audie. She now had five children and it would be impossible for her to support us. My grandpa had taken us in when it was just my mother and I, but even though he had a pretty decent job in the mines, he couldn't support all of us. It would have been an overwhelming task. This was more than likely the reason that my grandfather didn't do more than he did. I do believe to this day though, that if grandpa had known the extent of my situation that he would have found a way to intervene one way or another.

My grandpa always worked very hard. After the family moved to Pittsburg, he was a miner. Miners worked under pretty archaic conditions in those days. It was a very tough and sometimes dangerous job. There were many instances of accidents in which miners lost their lives down in the mines. They were very unsafe compared to today's standards of mine safety. Grandpa didn't get rich working in the mines, by any means, but he made enough to support himself and his family, which included my mother and me for a short period of time.

My grandfather didn't spend a whole lot of time involved in recreation because he didn't have much extra time after work and taking care of his family. When he did decide to try to have some fun, other than our excursions to town together, my grandfather did have a regular recreational activity that he enjoyed – gambling.

It was a pretty common activity in those days, as I notice that it still is today. In those days there were no floating gambling casinos in the area, or no trips to Vegas to play the slots. There may have been a goodly amount of betting on sporting events, races and such. I'm not really sure because these were not the forms of gambling that my grandfather participated in, at least to my knowledge. There was also a lot of gambling on card games and my grandfather loved to shoot dice.

It was pretty easy back in those days to find a place to gamble somewhere in our area. Grandpa usually found his share of them. I'm sure this took place much to the dismay of many wives of these participants. I'm not really sure what my grandma thought about my grandpa's gambling, but to my knowledge he in no way let it get in the way of his duties. Because of this fact, I really don't think he had a gambling addiction or anything like that. He just seemed to enjoy it. Nobody else in the family seemed to mind his gambling. At the time, however, we didn't realize that grandpa's occasional gambling would eventually lead to his untimely death.

Grandpa tried his luck at different locations in the area on occasion, but he had a favorite spot. On almost every Friday and Saturday night he would head to a farmhouse located between West Frankfort and Benton, Illinois, a few miles away from our home. I realize that it sounds hard to believe now, but back then if you had twenty dollars on you, you were considered well off. Even though twenty dollars was worth a lot more in those days, it could still disappear very quickly on a gambling run.

This spot like most other gambling facilities had plenty of alcohol on hand. This was one of the ways that a perspective gamer could quickly dispose of any winnings he had accumulated. Remember that at this time of prohibition, the sale and consumption of liquor was illegal. These players didn't let the law stand in their way of having a good time, at least what they thought was a good time.

As you can probably imagine, the mixture of gambling and alcohol was not a very good mix for many reasons. I'm sure there have been many a high roller enter the gaming establishment with his entire pay check in his pocket only to wake up early on a Sunday morning without a trace of it left to show for his night out. This undoubtedly made it a long week, or maybe two until the next pay day, especially if the participant had a family to support.

The illegal alcohol and the gaming in many instances brought in a very unseemly crowd. The bootleggers were usually local farmers who had a still and made the stuff themselves to share with their friends, or maybe sell. Sometimes people came in from out of the area and ended up at the card or dice game. Some of these people were there to gamble and sometimes they were there to try to fleece a local out of their winnings. They sometimes did this by swindling the man who had just come into some winnings while they were in an intoxicated condition. They also in some cases did not hesitate to use force to try to part these gamblers with their newfound lute. This could turn a rather innocent night out of playing cards or rolling the dice into a sometimes very dangerous situation. This setting apparently turned into a very dangerous situation for my grandfather.

My grandfather left one night headed to his usual gambling locale and he didn't return very early the next morning as he usually did. No one in the family seemed too worried at least at first. I imagine that my mom and grandma probably thought he had just had too much to drink and was sleeping if off somewhere. It would not be unusual for men in the area to do this, but it was unusual for my grandfather.

They may have thought that grandpa got too carried away on his gambling binge and lost so much that he was ashamed to come home to his family with the thought of losing money that could be used to support his family. This again would not have been too unusual for men in the area to have happen. Many men had found themselves flat broke and ashamed to face their family, if not afraid to incur the wrath of a furious wife who knew what the family would have to endure until the next paycheck. It's hard to blame the gambling man for avoiding this confrontation for as long as possible. This explanation would be very believable in some cases, but it was difficult to imagine this occurring in the case of my grandfather.

I remember asking about grandpa. I remember wondering where he was. I received a very cloudy explanation since I'm sure my mother and grandmother wanted to spare me the sorted details of my grandpa's gambling. It was another case of a child knowing more than adults give them credit for. I was aware of where my grandpa went on Friday and Saturday nights, very aware.

The real test of whether we had anything to worry about would come on Monday morning. There would be no way that grandpa would miss work if he was not in some kind of real trouble.

When Monday morning came and there was still no sign of my grandpa there was a definite change in attitude among the members of my family. This showed on their expressions. They tried not to show their apparent worry, but they were unsuccessful in their efforts to hide the fret in their thoughts.

My family looked around the area for him. They checked around with the usual participants at the farmhouse. There was no sign of him anywhere. At first, when he didn't show up, I think my grandmother was probably more upset with him than worried. It was one of those situations where you say "I hope he makes it home safely so that I can kill him." The person who makes the statement doesn't mean it, but it's how they feel at the moment.

After more than a week passed it was evident that one of two things had happened to my grandfather. He could have left the family for whatever reason. He had lost money and had become discouraged, or maybe he was just frustrated at the hard times and ran away from his troubles. This happened quite often. Some distraught people in the stock market on Wall Street responded to the crash of the market and the onset of the great depression by jumping out of windows of tall buildings. Some destitute men in Southern Illinois responded by running out on their families.

This at first glance sounded like one of the most cruel and cowardly acts possible. Even though I don't agree with their thinking, some men believed that their families would be better off without them. They thought that the family could get some kind of assistance if they were without a "breadwinner". I believe that even though this could in some cases be true, that this thinking is flawed. In my opinion in these very difficult times we faced, the presence of a father meant more to a family than any amount of money could offset. Whereas I don't agree with their decision, I understand why they did it and would not condemn any man for choosing this option even though I still believe it was a tragic mistake.

The other option was that my grandfather was involved in some kind of foul play. This happened sometimes in the exchange of what sometimes was very large sums of money. Sometimes there were arguments over aspects of the circumstances of the games themselves. Was someone cheating or doing something to gain an advantage? I'm sure that sometimes there was some unfair cheating going on and sometimes it was just "sour grapes" at the loss of a gamblers hard earned money.

I just could never for one-second fathom that my grandpa would ever abandon us. This left only one option, the latter one. We had hoped that we were wrong, unfortunately we were not.

After ten days had passed since the mysterious disappearance of my grandpa we finally received the news that we had dreaded for several days. We got word that a body had been found in a rural area about a half a mile north of West Frankfort. We had hoped that it was not grandpa, but it unfortunately was. A train engineer had noticed the body of my grandfather floating in a creek along a rural area of tracks between the farmhouse and my grandfather's home. There was no identification or anything to identify my grandpa, but we eventually got the official sad news that it was him.

The authorities reasoned that he had been dead for several days since the body had decomposed to an extent in which it would have been difficult to identify him without close inspection. He also had no wallet or any kind of money anywhere on him.

Putting these things together it was pretty evident that grandpa had been robbed on his way home from the card, or dice game that he had participated in. One of the reasons that my grandpa loved to gamble was because he was pretty good at it. He more often than not left the game with more money than he entered with. He more than likely had some winnings on his person that night when he left the farmhouse. He was probably followed home by someone, or more than one, and attacked. This is obviously just speculation, but I'm satisfied that even though we don't know the exact details of the assault, it happened along these lines in some scenario. The crime, however, was never solved.

It didn't really matter to me how the crime actually took place, all I knew was that my beloved grandpa was gone for good. The only person, who really seemed to love me, at least the only one that showed it, was no longer around. I was devastated. I was hurt more deeply than I even believed I could be hurt. I had believed that grandpa would always be there for me. He was the only reason that I made it up to that point in my childhood and I would now have to face life without him. For a time period, I honestly did not want to go on. I missed him deeply.

Things were a lot different in many ways for me after the passing of my grandpa. I no longer had that one person who cared about me to lean on. I no longer had the one person who was actually proud of me. I no longer had what at that time was my best friend. It was without a doubt one of the toughest periods in my life.

As much time passed I eventually came to grips with grandpa's death. I guess the fact that I was very young at the time helped in this process. I never really got over the emptiness that I felt, but I moved on. Even then I seemed to be resilient in dealing with difficult and sometimes very emotional aspects of life in general. It has continued to serve me well as I make it down life's pathway. I still missed him, but I found myself remembering the good times we had together and feeling fortunate to have had my grandfather for the time that I did.

One of the most dramatic differences in my life after the passing of grandpa was the relationship between my father and me. It was an opportunity for my father to change his ways. He had a glowing opportunity to try to reestablish his fatherly presence in my life. He could have gone a long way in filling the void left by my grandfather's passing – but he didn't.

Actually just the opposite happened. It may sound difficult to believe, but my relationship with my father actually deteriorated drastically after my grandfather was gone.

With my grandpa gone, I found myself in the grips of depression. At that time, it sure didn't seem like life had much in store for me. It seemed like I had no one who really cared about me. My parents continued their unloving treatment of me, no matter how hard I worked to please them. I somehow continued to treat them with respect, but it was difficult to do.

I had lost my beloved grandpa and I found myself wishing I were dead. For a time period it felt like the most appealing option. I don't really remember actually contemplating suicide, thank God, but I vividly remember wishing that my life would end, because in my mind it had already essentially ended with my grandpa's passing. I thought I had nothing to live for. At the time I didn't realize that this was wrong. This was so very wrong.

Chapter 3

As my emotional frame of mind was battered and torn by the death of grandpa, the financial standing of our family was, if possible, in an even more desperate state. Things in Southern Illinois continued to be extremely economically depressed in the early 1930's. Jobs were scarce and money was hard to come by.

My dad continued to make his living, as meager as it was, by manufacturing his own homemade bootleg liquor at his own still. He had it set up back about a mile into the heavy woods and out of sight. If he were caught bootlegging, he would be sent to prison, so he had to be very discreet. He had a group of "regulars" that frequented his small farm brewery. Many people knew about my father's still and other stills as well, but they kept quiet because they knew if the bootleggers were caught that it would shut down the still. This would cut off the supply of moonshine in the local area. My father also continued to take in his share of his creation, which made things even more difficult.

One day when I was about six years old, I was outside playing with my little brother, Henry. It was very early in the morning and Henry and I were the only children who were old enough to be allowed to play outside by ourselves. My mother and the rest of the kids were inside, while my dad was already out in the woods at the still getting a batch of moonshine going.

Two men suddenly approached my brother and me. I didn't recognize either of them. They were not among the regulars that frequented dad's still. Besides, it was awfully early to start drinking, though I guess it seemed like some of the local men drank pretty much around the clock. The two men asked us where they could find our father, Audie Rains.

My father had anticipated just such an occurrence, so he had always told us that if anyone came to the house looking for him to tell them that we didn't know where he was. Before I could get the words out of my mouth, my little brother had already pointed toward the woods. The men, who turned out to be federal men, then headed toward the wooded area by our house.

As the men headed away I was petrified. At the time I didn't even know for sure that the men wanted to cause any trouble for my dad. I still thought that it was possible that they might be new customers. The reason I was so terrified was that we had disobeyed my father's orders not to tell anyone where he was when he was operating the still. Even though it was actually my brother, Henry who had pointed them in the direction of the still and not me, I knew who would likely get the blame for it.

I thought that the men might not even find dad as far back into the woods as he was. They must have followed dad's footprints in the morning dew, because they tracked him down. They took my father in on a charge of making illegal bootleg liquor.

We didn't see my father again until his trial in Benton. It was a very short trial and my father was found guilty of bootlegging. He was sentenced to six months at the Vandalia Correctional Institution.

My dad's income that he had been taking in from the still was now gone. This made it almost impossible for my mother to feed the family. Luckily we didn't have to worry about not having my father around for very long, not even the six months that he had been given.

My mother made the trip up to Vandalia to visit her husband on occasion. We were never allowed to go along. On one visit while my mother and father were visiting I guess they decided to get a little daring. Maybe my father had had enough of this prison life and decided to try to get out of there before his time was up. It didn't really make too much sense looking back because dad's time would have been up in a short period of time, but they made the attempt any way.

It would be more exciting if I could tell you that my parents had come up with some ingenious plan to dupe the guards, or overpower them by the use of some well thought out scheme. The truth is that all that happened was that my father seemed to notice that the guards were not paying too much attention to my parents as they visited, so he decided to try to make his way out with my mother as she left. I'm sure you're thinking that this could never work. The guards would surely be too watchful to let something as simple as this result in a prison escape. They weren't.

My father just walked right out of there with my mother and no one noticed it. I guess the guards didn't figure that any one with such a light sentence would risk a longer stay, or more frightful yet, a transfer to a maximum-security facility with a more hardened group of inmates. My parents and my father in particular decided to risk the repercussions and make a run for it. Looking back, it probably wasn't the smartest thing to risk it with so little time left, but it worked none the less.

It didn't take long for word to get out of my father's prison break. There was now a massive search on for him. My mother had avoided any implication of guilt. I guess they never did figure out that dad just walked out with her. Because of this my father could not risk returning home to Southern Illinois. He had some family down south in Kentucky, so he made his way down there and was hiding out until the search for him died down in the area.

After my father got settled down in Kentucky, he sent for us to come and join him there. When we arrived we slowly made our way out into the middle of a deserted cornfield where there was what a simple structure that looked like it could be considered a shack at best. There were no windows and no doors. There were only burlap cloths where the doors and windows once were. It in no way shape or form resembled an abode in which someone would actually set up housekeeping - we did.

When I say out in the middle of nowhere, I really mean it. There was no one around us, it seemed for miles. Even though we were now out of state and the search had died down somewhat for my dad, they still didn't think it was safe for us to wonder too far from the shack that we were currently calling home.

We also had almost no money. My father had not been able to regroup and set up a still, so we had no income. Because of this we could not afford to buy any food. We survived, barely, by living off of the land. We ate mostly corn and things that my mother could make from the grain. Things were so desperate that we also had very little water, which we garnered, from a creek not too far away from our home. It was a pitiful existence for all of us. We had thought that we had very little back in Illinois, but we were now quite literally on the brink of starvation.

The lack of food for the time period we spent in Kentucky took its toll on all of us. It was very difficult watching what it was doing to my mother and my siblings. There's not too much more agonizing than watching a youngster not have enough to eat. We all were starting to show the signs of our lack of food and nutrition, so much so that when some family members visited our shack. They were appalled and encouraged us to get out of there.

After a time period, my father decided that it was safe to return home to Pittsburg, Illinois. He believed that enough time had passed that authorities had likely suspended their search for him. I guess he thought that the law had better things to do than spend valuable time and man force looking for an escaped bootlegger. I sure was relieved to get out of that old shack and head back home. I was relieved, but the relief seemed only to last for a short time.

Chapter 4

During the time I was growing up, I usually didn't have much if any free time. I was usually doing some type of work and didn't have time for very much else. My siblings played games and such, but I usually didn't have time to take part. The things that kids did back then would seem very simple to today's standards. Life was pretty laid back and simple in Southern Illinois in the thirties, and there wasn't really too much for a youngster to do that would be considered exciting.

The only form of regular entertainment we had in town was the movie house. It opened on Saturday afternoons and all the kids in town would go and watch a movie. It was the era of silent films, so there was no sound. It seems kind of funny today considering all the advances they have made in movie making technology. As I remember, we watched a lot of "Cowboy and Indian" type shows. I always looked forward to it.

There was another regular form of recreation in town, but it was mainly for adults. Almost every Saturday night, weather permitting, there would be a dance. The adults would square dance in the streets. There was some really good music and the adults seemed to really enjoy it. It gave them a chance to forget their troubles for a few hours.

Another of the few recreational things that I really recall from my early childhood was when the "gypsies" would come to town. They usually traveled in a large caravan of beautifully painted covered wagons. The wagons would have very elaborate paintings of murals on them. They were extremely beautiful. They would set up camp just outside of town. This would cause a stir in Pittsburg for several reasons.

One of our society's greatest problems has been that of stereotyping. We see an instance of one, or maybe a few members of a group of people's behavior, good or bad, and it is attributed to the entire race of people. This travesty sure has been a huge stumbling block in our society's attempts at improving relations among peoples of different race. With what I would see and be a part of in my later service in World War II, I would never want to be guilty of any unfair labeling or stereotyping, but regardless of this fact, most people in our area did not trust the gypsies.

People in general seemed to classify all gypsies as thieves. When the gypsies would arrive, people would go all over town alerting the townspeople. Most everyone around the area would lock up their livestock and their homes.

There were all kinds of rumors floating around about the gypsies. We used to hear that they would steal livestock and raid people's gardens for food. We also used to hear that they would actually steal children from the towns that they frequented and sell them, or maybe use them in their carnival or medicine show.

After hearing all these frightening stories about them, I was pretty scared of them. I used to get up the nerve to go to their camp and sell them blackberries. I have to admit that it was kind of spooky, mainly I think because they did not speak English, so I was never sure what they were saying. I used to wonder in my mind if they were contemplating grabbing my blackberries and me and hauling me off to perform in some show.

I never in all the times that I visited their camps had any trouble with any of the gypsies. I imagine that it's like any other instance of labeling a group of people. There were probably some members of the gypsy community who may have been guilty of the offenses that they were accused of in the rumors we used to hear, but it probably was very exaggerated. It's really hard to blame the townspeople, though. There was no law in our little town, so they had to really be on guard if they believed there was any potential threat to their family or their belongings. Because of this fact they were probably a little quick to overreact. I actually used to look forward to the gypsies coming to town. Their carnival and shows, when I was fortunate enough to go, were very entertaining. It was one of the few forms of entertainment that my siblings and I got a chance to take in back in those days.

If it wasn't Saturday afternoon and the gypsies weren't in town then we had to be more creative to find something to do during our free time. I didn't really become close to a lot of other boys in the area because I was usually working instead of playing with them. Because of this, I sometimes felt like an outsider, so to speak, when I would get an opportunity to try to have some fun.

I had been given the job of caretaker of my brothers when we were out and about in town. I was supposed to make sure that they stayed out of trouble and that no one harmed them. They usually accompanied me when we would look for something to do around the area.

As you can imagine in a group of what was predominately young boys without much to do, there would occasionally be trouble. If there was some kind of dispute a fight might break out at any moment. More often than not though, the fight was not a result of any other dispute, the fight broke out because it was fun, at least for some of the youngsters. Boys would challenge each other's manhood by trying to see who was the toughest combatant. I had to make sure that my brothers stayed out of any of these fracases. I knew that I would be in for trouble at home if they got hurt, or even dirty in an altercation. My parents never allowed me to fight. If I came home after a fight with torn or dirty clothes I would have a date with a razor strap.

The only way that I was allowed to fight would be if I were defending my brothers during some kind of dispute. I was a pretty tough young lad in those days. I guess it was because I had been forced to work very hard from a young age and had developed my share of strength and endurance compared to most kids my age.

I had developed somewhat of a reputation of being tough. This caused a lot of the other boys to want to challenge me to a fight. I always declined. This usually made the boy mad. I would be insulted by being called names as the youngster tried to provoke me. Sometimes I would even be pushed or even hit by the would-be fighter. The other kids were always amazed that I could keep my temper and resist socking the kid who was dishing it out to me. It really wasn't that I had such great control of my temper, it was more that I knew what the razor strap could do to me. I knew that that's exactly what I would be in for when I got home if I gave in and participated in the altercation. I would gladly take the insults and the occasional strikes of a young boy verses facing a razor strap.

It didn't take long for the boys around town to figure out how they could get me into a fight. All they had to do was grab one of my brothers. This was the only way I could get involved in the fight. This happened many times after they figured this out. I remember one incident in particular.

On one occasion a boy that was about the same size as me wanted to try me out. I refused. He continued to try to provoke me into an altercation. I still declined knowing what I would face when I got home. By this time a pretty big crowd had gathered around. They were all trying to throw fuel on the fire by their taunts. They wanted to see the free entertainment of a fight breaking out. There was also an adult who was there hoping to see some combat. A local bread and cake deliveryman had noticed the possible skirmish while making a drop off at the local general store in town. He stopped by and offered a dozen day-old donuts to the winner of the fight.

I have to admit that it was tempting. Donuts were a treat that we didn't get to partake of very often. They sure sounded good, but I still refused. I hadn't forgot what would be waiting for me when I got home. No matter how tasty those donuts would have been, they weren't worth taking a licking with the razor strap for.

Finally one of the on-lookers that was familiar with my situation took the boy aside to give him some advice. The boy then realized how he could indeed get me to fight. He approached my little brother, Audie Ray and grabbed him by the neck. The fight was on. I managed to get the first punch in and knocked him down to the ground. The boy regrouped himself and got up. Before he could ready himself, I hit him again. He fell to the ground for the second time. After a moment he got up again. He was definitely a little woozy from the two blows and he was an easy target for my third and final strike. I hit him probably even harder than I had hit him the first two times. He stayed down this time and gave up.

The donut man approached me after the boy didn't get up the third time. He congratulated me and offered me the dozen donuts. I declined to accept his offer of the treat. It had come to me as I was involved in the altercation that I was fighting to protect my brother and not for anyone else's satisfaction. I wasn't fighting to provide free entertainment for the crowd that had gathered on that day, and certainly not for a treat, as nice as it would have been to eat those donuts. I told the donut man this, as I refused his treats. I think he was pretty surprised. I'm sure the kids watching thought I was crazy not to accept the sweets, but I think I had learned something that day that some people don't learn until much later on in life. There are things in life that should be done whether you are personally rewarded for them, or not. If your motivation for fighting is some kind of personal reward, then you miss the point of why you're fighting. I would learn much more about this later in my life.

It the midst of all my personal troubles during my childhood, I did have the opportunity to learn some valuable lessons about helping and caring for people. I felt a little bit of this myself, since I found myself caring for my brothers and my sister some. There was one particular day when my brother cared for me.

I used to do what I could to help the family get extra money when possible. The most prominent way that I accomplished this was the selling of blackberries. I would pick a good amount of the berries and then pack them up and take them to Marion. I would then go house to house selling them for twenty-five cents a gallon. I know it doesn't sound like much, but back then it helped out a lot.

Sometimes my little brother, Henry would accompany me. I had picked a load of blackberries and was on my way to Marion to try to peddle them. It was about a six-mile walk to Marion, which wasn't an easy trek on a cool day. This particular day was in late July and it was brutally hot outside. As anyone who has been to Southern Illinois in late July knows the humidity was also very high which made things even worse. I had sold the berries and we were on our way back home from Marion at just about midday. I started feeling a little funny, and then all of a sudden I don't remember what happened. I learned later that I had passed out.

I had defended and taken care of my brother a lot of times in the past, but this time he took care of me. He quickly rolled me under a shade tree to keep the blazing sun from shining down on me.

He then found a ditch that had a small amount of water in it. He took the water from the ditch and put it on my forehead to cool me down. He did this for over thirty minutes before I finally came to. It was pretty good thinking for a person of any age to deal with a sudden illness like that, but especially for my brother who was only six years old at the time. I was still in a very weak condition as he then helped me back home to Pittsburg. We found out later after describing the incident, that I had probably had a heat stroke. If my brother had not been there that day, I might well have died. I will always be grateful to him for his help. It was one of many instances in which someone intervened to spare my life.

Along with my brothers and sister, I also felt a little responsible for my mother since I felt like the reason that she had problems with my stepfather was because of me. Because of this I was very protective of her. In the spring of 1937 I learned even more about the importance of helping people in need.

In 1937 there was a heavy snowfall in our area. In the spring months, as the snow was melting and had saturated the ground, we also had some bouts of very heavy rains. Because of this the Mississippi and Ohio Rivers were overflowing their flood stages. This caused major flooding in Indiana, Kentucky, Missouri, and in my Southern Illinois home. Towns were under water as much as twenty miles from the riverbanks. Almost all the "river towns" were completely flooded in Southern Illinois. The Pittsburg area was flooded, but not as badly as some of the area towns were. We had approximately two feet of water covering our land. If any of you have lived through a flood, you know how difficult it is to clean up after the waters rescind. We had it bad enough, but not as tough as some people from neighboring towns. Many of the people in the towns along the river, like Harrisburg, Shawneetown, or Golconda, were forced to evacuate their homes completely.

The government had to use boats to rescue people and sometimes-even animals from these flooded towns. They hired my stepfather, along with many other men around Southern Illinois with boats to aid in this process. It was kind of ironic that the government was hiring my father, since he was, in fact, an escaped prisoner. I guess they either didn't know, or maybe didn't care. I'm not sure which.

Because of the flood of 1937, many people lost a lot. Some people lost almost all of their belongings to the water disaster. A massive operation was started to help the victims of the flooding. Many people from all over the country donated things to families that had lost all their belongings. It was incredible to see that people from all around the United States wanted to help us.

We were not as unfortunate as many families in Southern Illinois, but we did qualify to receive some of the donated items. We didn't have much before the flood, let alone after. As I looked through the donated clothing, I found a pair of pants that fit me very nicely. As I was trying them on, I reached into the pocket of the pants and found something. It was a note. The note was from a boy about my age and size who was from Pennsylvania. He asked in his note for the recipient of the pants that he had donated, to write him a letter telling him what it was like to have lived through the flood.

I managed to scrape up a penny some where and wrote to the boy in Pennsylvania on a one-cent postcard. I told him about the flood and what it was like to have lived through it for a boy our age. I told him that it had been miserable and that he was fortunate not to have to experience the disaster. He wrote back and thanked me for the letter. He told me a little about himself. We wrote back and forth to each other a few times. We eventually ended our correspondence and I never heard from the boy again.

I would not want to have to live through that flood of 1937 again, but I did learn a lot from it. It was nice to see the people in the area work together to help each other deal with the effects of the massive flood. It was also especially nice to see that a boy in Pennsylvania, who didn't know me, or anyone else he might be helping, would lend his help by sending clothing. It made me feel very good and taught me that even though it seemed sometimes that people were hard hearted, that most people were very kind. It made it easier for me to be kind and respectful even when I was being mistreated. It was one of many things that happened to me during my childhood that taught me about people.

Chapter 5

There were not too many ways to make a good living in Southern Illinois during the depression riddled thirties. Many families lived on farms and tried to make a living this way. Times were difficult though, and prices for crops were down. Because of this many families lost their farms and everything they owned. Probably the most stable form of income in the area was found in the mines. Mine companies were trying to pump out as much coal as they could sell for fuel. This caused the mines to keep many men employed during the time period.

Having a job at the mines was lucrative for a few reasons. It was one of only a few steady forms of income in the area. As compared to farming, a man didn't have to worry about grain prices and such. You knew you were getting a paycheck each week, which during the depression was hard to come by. It also paid pretty well compared to most occupations in the area. Many of the small factories that at one time could have competed with the mine's wages had closed because of the depression's onset. Any man that had a steady, well-paying job in that time was considered fortunate.

There were also some reasons that working in the mines could not be considered a good thing. It was in many ways a difficult job. There was not the machinery that exists today to help the mining process. Much of what is today done with massive machinery was done by hand. It was tough. Mining is also inherently dangerous. It's still considered dangerous today, but it was much more so back in those days. There were many instances of miners losing their lives in accidents at various mines throughout the Southern Illinois area.

Everyone pretty much realized that working in the mines could be dangerous, at best. Many people though, believed that the mines were made even more dangerous than they could be. There was a big call for the owners of the mining companies to do everything they could to make the mines safer. Many people at that time believed that the mine companies were ignoring many things that could be done to make the mines safer for the miners. The companies didn't seem to be too worried about the protest. It seemed as if the miners had no leverage to try to improve conditions at the mines. The miners were kind of over a barrel, so to speak. The mining companies knew that the miners needed to work to support their families during this critical financial time. They also knew that if they caused too much of a stir that the mine could easily get rid of them and find hundreds of men that would be willing to work under those conditions to receive that much-coveted paycheck to help support their family. These factors help cause a push for a union in the mines to represent the workers.

Living right next to the mine in Pittsburg, we were witness to some of these goings on concerning the mines. Some people wanted the union and some didn't. It wasn't that the group opposed to the union didn't want better working conditions. They were in most cases just afraid of losing their jobs. They probably didn't feel like it was worth risking being out of work for. I'm sure they felt as if they couldn't fight the big mine companies on their own. These conditions opened the door for the entrance of the gangs to jump into the picture on behalf of the workers.

Gangs had been very prominent in Southern Illinois even before the depression. They did, however, seem to prosper during the depression. After the economic troubles began many banks and businesses had been forced to close their doors. Many people who had had plenty of money up to that point had lost it all. Many people, especially farmers had started their own small-time bootlegging operation. Because of prohibition, this had become an appealing way to make a living. Since it was illegal, bootleggers had to be very discrete about their set up. To help each other avoid the law and prosecution, gangs were formed. These gangs would find remote places around Southern Illinois where water and corn, which were essential to the bootlegging process, was plentiful. The gangs would help protect the operation of the still and they were rewarded by payment, sometimes by money and more often by bootleg liquor.

There were two gangs that had become notorious in Southern Illinois. There were many more, but these were the most influential and well known of them. One of these more prominent gangs was the Shelton gang. They operated out of Fairfield. They made and sold bootleg liquor up and down the Wabash River near the Indiana border on the eastern part of Southern Illinois. The other prominent gang in the area was the Burger gang. They were headquartered between Marion and Harrisburg, not too far from where I grew up. Charlie Burger founded the gang. He was no longer around after having been executed for his crimes. He was hanged on the Town Square in Benton, Illinois. It was the last public hanging in the area that I am aware of. The gang he formed was still very active.

The gangs were determined to form a union in the mines. At first glance it might seem as if the gangs were trying to promote the interests of the miners. After all the miners were forced to work in very unsafe conditions. They were in a sense at the mercy of the coal companies because of their financial condition. The fact of some group being formed to help defend their interests was very appealing. Unfortunately, the gangs were concerned more with the money they could make from the dues they would be collecting than the safety of the miners.

The gangs jumped in and tried to solidify itself as a bargaining unit for the coal miners. As you can probably guess the mine companies scoffed at this proposal. They obviously refused to recognize the unions formed by the gangs. The gangs then worked to try to form strikes at local mines determined to force the mine companies to recognize them.

The gangs worked tirelessly spreading union propaganda in the area and trying to persuade individual miners to become part of the striking force. A strike would be pretty much useless unless the vast majority of miners participated. As I mentioned earlier, many of the miners didn't want a union. As you can probably imagine, the gangs found ways to convince the miners to change their mind on the issue.

The gangs could be very "persuasive". They would meet workers as they came out of the mines and try to convince them to become a part of the union and the planned strike against the coal companies. If the worker agreed with the gang's proposal there was no problem. If they didn't agree, and sometimes they didn't, then there was definitely trouble.

If a miner crossed the picket line and went into work while the gang ordered strike was under way, they were targeted. Sometimes, if they were lucky, the miner was given another chance to reconsider and sometimes they weren't. There were several instances of crossing miners being found the next morning with a bullet in their head.

We also were witness to another way the gang sent their message to miners not to cross the picket line. We lived in what was referred to as Colp Patch, which was a housing area built by Colp Coal

Company. It was only about seven hundred feet from their mine, so we could see the activities at the mine.

There was a very large oak tree in our area. We always walked by it on our way to and from school. On more than one occasion we had to walk by dead men swinging from that old oak tree. It served as a very chilling reminder to the miners and also their families that they better not cross the gangs. On several nights I can remember lying in bed and hearing that oak tree crying. It sounded like a man crying. It was pretty spooky. I don't know if it was the wind blowing through the tree, or what, but to this day I can remember hearing it clear as a bell. The gangs had succeeded in getting their message across to the people in the area.

I didn't have too many direct dealings with gang members. There was one occasion in which I got to see and interact with gang members. I was walking from my home in Pittsburg to Marion. I was going there to sell blackberries, which as I mentioned I did whenever I could to make some extra money for the family. As I made my way down the road, I was hitchhiking. Some days I got picked up and some days I didn't. On this particular day I got picked up, all right. Three members of the Burger gang picked me up.

When the car stopped and I got inside, I didn't notice any difference between the members of the car I was riding in and the people who I had gotten rides with before. The first thing that made me realize that there was indeed something different about these men, was the appearance of two machine guns. There was one in the front seat and one in the back seat where I was sitting. I didn't see all their weapons, but I'm fairly confident that each gang member was probably carrying a gun with them also, so they were definitely well armed.

I was a little startled for a moment when I first saw the artillery in the car, but the feeling didn't last long. The men were extremely nice to me. They talked a lot. They seemed to be interested in me, and what I was doing with all those blackberries. They were extremely nice to me during the ride to Marion and I never felt the least bit threatened. In fact, I didn't even realize who they were until later when I would witness what they had come to Marion to do.

After I got out of the car in Marion and said my thanks and good-byes, the gang car pulled up in front of the Williamson County Courthouse. They got out of the car in front of the courthouse located in Marion. They then proceeded to grab a megaphone and called out the police department. They actually had the nerve, and I guess the confidence to call out the police department in broad daylight in the middle of town. They were not the least bit frightened of the police. As is turns out, they apparently had nothing to be afraid of because they stayed there for about ten minutes or so and there was absolutely no response from the police department at all. As many people looked on, the gang members moved on. They definitely sent the message that they had intended to send. I'm sure the people who witnessed this act were extremely intimidated, as were the police. I was absolutely amazed. I couldn't believe that the police would actually let those gang members drive right up to the Town Square, and more or less taunt them. I don't believe I knew what to think at that moment. I actually found myself liking the men I had ridden with, but I also remember feeling a little let down by the fact that someone like that could get away with doing something like that to our police department. I don't think I felt quite as safe after seeing that site. It was very unsettling, very unsettling, indeed.

Chapter 6

Life in the Rains' household was not getting any better for me, if anything, as difficult as it might seem, it was getting worse. I had even more household chores than ever before. I also never seemed to be able to please anyone with the way I went about trying to obey my burdensome orders. Then I found out something that would change my life, totally.

After a dispute with my father, I took off and was running through the area crying hysterically. I made my way through the neighborhood. About a quarter of a mile from home, a neighbor lady stopped me. She had known my family and me all of my life. She looked me over and asked me what was wrong. I then proceeded to tell her what had happened. She paused for a moment. I'm sure that she knew that this was not only a one-time occurrence. I think she was well aware of what I had to go through.

She then asked me why I didn't leave home and go to live with my "real" dad. I didn't know what she meant. I had no idea what she was talking about. What did she mean "real dad"? I had a dad. He was my real dad, wasn't he? – He wasn't.

The woman didn't go into all the details, but she then said that she had the name and address of my father, if I wanted to try to contact him about going to be with him. This had really happened too fast. A trusted family friend and neighbor was seemingly telling me that the man, who I had called dad since I was an infant, was not my real father. It was difficult for me to understand.

In retrospect, I didn't really understand the details of what this newfound information had brought to me. It did answer a lot of questions in my mind, though. I had always wondered why he had treated me so very differently than the other kids. I also wondered why he was so tough on me. I now knew. I was not his son, after all. I didn't really realize it completely then, but I guess he had not accepted me as his child knowing that my mother had slept with another man and that I was the product of this relationship.

If I had had more time to think about her offer, I might have responded differently, but I declined the lady's information. I knew that if I made it known that I had learned about this information after all these years that my stepfather would not appreciate it. He would have made things even more difficult on me, and to me even more importantly I believed things would be more difficult for my mother. I declined the offer of my father's name and address, though years later I sometimes wondered how my life would have been different had I not turned down her offer.

Things seemed to be getting even more difficult for my mother, also. She had me and four other children to try to corral which was a mountainous task in the best of circumstances. She definitely was not in the best of circumstances. Times were tough and there was a lot of pressure on the both of them as they tried to make ends meet.

One day I got into a confrontation with my father. My mother was just about hysterical. She said to run away and not to come back. I ran and just kept running. I ran away from home. I felt as if I had no other choice.

I had looked out for my mother for many years. I did it in a time in a youngster's life in which that's usually the last thing to worry about. In most families, in fact, in works just the opposite. Most of the time a child feels like his mother, in particular, is looking out for them. This is the way it's supposed to be, but it wasn't for me. I didn't really ever feel as if my mother was looking out for me, I felt as if I was looking out for her. I guess I was continuing this because I was causing her more trouble by being there, so I left. In my way of thinking I was actually continuing to look out for her even though I wasn't there.

Like in any situation in which a youngster bolts his home to run away, I had many second thoughts after I got several miles away. I started to question my thinking. After all, it didn't seem like the smartest thing to do. I had no food, no place to stay, and the only clothes I had were the clothes on my back. I had no means to garner any of these items that I needed to survive.

For several days I just wondered around, not really knowing what it was I should do. I kept questioning and then requestioning my decision to leave home. I decided a few times to go back only to rethink my change of heart and stay away from home. It was a very tough time for me. I felt very lonely as I wondered around. I knew I had to find some means of support to buy food and to find a place to stay. I decided to try to find a job.

I thought I could find a job easily enough. I figured that someone would hire me. I would work hard and I would work cheap. Surely someone would hire a strong young kid who was willing to work.

Boy, was I wrong. I checked around almost everywhere and nobody would hire me. They had various reasons, but no one wanted to give me a job. I guess it was mainly my age. If they did in fact have work available, there was more than a fair amount of grown men who would be more than happy to accept the employment, what with times being so tough. Also, most of the places of employment weren't hiring anybody, period, no matter the age of the applicant. No matter the reasoning, the important thing was that I still had no food, clothing, or shelter and no money to solve my need.

After exhausting all the potential employment opportunities in the immediate area, I decided to expand my search. My mom's brother, my Uncle John Hayes had moved about the area by hopping freight trains. He used it as a common means of travel. He had managed to pass this art onto me. I decided to make use of my skill. I went to Marion and caught the first freight train that came through town.

I rode the northbound train for about 250 miles. I got off in an area in Northern Illinois, near Decatur. I departed the train in a rural area in what seemed in the middle of nowhere. As I was making my way toward what I thought would be the most likely direction of a town, I heard some voices. I paused for a moment to see where they were coming from. They were coming from a wooded area just off into the distance. I carefully approached the direction where the sound was coming, being careful not to give myself away.

As I got closer to the woods I started to smell food. It's always appealing to smell food cooking, but as hungry as I was at that moment, I think it actually made my mouth water. I thought that I had probably wondered on to a country church that was having a picnic, social, or some kind of dinner. The aroma drew me closer and closer. I hoped that the members of this church would be gracious to a hungry wondering soul. As I finally got to a point where I could see beyond the clearing, I could already taste the juicy morsels that were cooking. Much to my surprise, I found that this was no church and there was no social going on there, either.

I had stumbled onto a hobo camp. "Hobos" were men who, like me, were out of work and trying to use all means possible to survive. They usually traveled, again like me, by train, which was the reason that I happened onto their camp. These men would set up these camps and work together, somewhat to help each other survive. They would live off the land and do just about whatever it took to get food into their mouths and clothes on their backs. They usually built some kind of primitive types of shelters, like lean-tos and such.

One of the men noticed me and offered me something to eat. Normally I wouldn't have been all that anxious to partake in rabbit stew and such, but at this point I would have eaten just about anything. I would learn later that it was difficult to imagine to what means a man would go to get something to eat if he's desperate enough. The food actually tasted great, at least to me it did.

The men of the hobo camp were extremely nice to me. They seemed to get a real kick out of taking me under their wing, so to speak. I heard many stories from several different men of the camp about what they had had to do to survive. Most of the men were at one time very upstanding citizens in their community.

The same thing happened to most of the men that had happened to many men at the time, they had lost their job. Some of them had no families, but many of them did. They either had left home to find work and send money back to help their wives and families, or they were too embarrassed at the loss of their livelihood to face their family. It was a tough time financially for many. These men had just decided to handle the tough times in a little different method. It was their way of survival.

I traveled with the group for several days. It was rather comforting. I now had several men looking out for my survival and me. It made me feel pretty good. They made sure I was fed and taken care of. They let me bunk down with them and always made sure I was near the fire especially on cool nights. Maybe it made me feel particularly good to have the attention of the men because of the relationship between my dad and me. I don't know for sure.

Another aspect of the men of the hobo camp that intrigued me was their approach to alcohol. Almost all of the men drank some type of liquor. It was usually a cheap homemade version. I guess like many of the men in society at this time, the hobos used the alcohol to help them forget their troubles. The thing that fascinated me the most was their approach to alcohol concerning me. In all the many times I saw the men drinking alcohol during my stay at the hobo camp not one man offered me anything to drink. I figured they were all looking out for my well being. It made me feel good at the time and looking back I greatly appreciate the men taking this approach with an impressionable youngster.

One of the things that I liked best about life in the hobo camp was the entertainment. Most of the men had musical instruments and many were very talented musicians. They would play wonderful music almost every night.

There was, however, a sad side to the musical entertainment. The men usually played during the evening and into bedtime. On many nights I lay in my makeshift bed and listened to the songs. The men knew many songs that had a sad twist to them. As the men played I would think about the sad songs. It would make me reflect on my life. I thought a lot about my family and the trouble that I had had during my childhood. I thought of my mother and my siblings and how much I missed them. As I pondered these things, I got very sad, so sad that I would cry. I made sure that I didn't let any of the men see me cry. I was embarrassed. I didn't want them to think that I was a crybaby or anything like that. This sure was a sign of immaturity on my part. I learned later that it was no shame for a man to shed tears. Later in my life I would witness many men weep on the battlefield and I also shed more than my share of tears in many instances. I learned that we should never be ashamed to show our emotions, especially to the people in life that we care the most about.

We would jump trains and travel all around the area. We had to be rather elusive since the railroad had employed inspectors who would search the trains for men like us. With things as tough economically as they were, more and more men were using this method to travel around looking for employment, not all of them hobos. These inspectors were pretty rough on the hobos if caught. We had to carefully board the train and get off just before it reached the next town. I have to admit it was kind of exciting, but I knew it was not the way I wanted to spend my life. As much as I enjoyed the company of the men and security that traveling in a group brought, I knew I eventually had to find legitimate employment and get on with my life.

After having jumped off the train, I was walking through the nearest town. As I was wondering around the town looking for work, I noticed a group of boys looking at a sign in a store window. They read the sign and didn't seem the least bit interested in it.

The sign advertised that the United States Department of Agriculture was starting a program to put young men sixteen and over to work. It was called the Civilian Conservation Corp. Camp, or C.C.C. Camp. It was billed as sort of an army training ground, which was probably why the other boys showed little interest. It might not sound too appealing, but it was a means of support, which was something that I didn't have at the moment. There was only one problem. I was just short of fourteen years old at the time.

Enough time had passed for me to brave going back home to try to get my parents to tell the C.C.C. that I was two years older than I actually was. My father had long cooled down from the incident that caused me to leave home. I was around long enough though, to see that things had not changed too much around the Rains' house. They wrote a note saying that my year of birth was 1923, which was actually three years earlier than my actual year of birth, 1926.

I needed the note because I had no real birth certificate to verify my age. I took the note to the officials at the C.C.C. They wouldn't accept their word. They said that if I could get a note from the doctor, who attended to me at birth, stating the year I was born then they would accept it and allow me entrance into the camp.

My family had always been rather friendly with a local doctor from Pittsburg. He was a good doctor and an extremely nice person. He would make house calls, going to the homes of his patients when they needed medical treatment. He would also take just about anything for payment. This fact would come in handy in my dealings with the doctor.

There was also one other characteristic that would become important in dealing with this doctor. He, like many other men at the time, liked his whiskey. Knowing this, I approached the good doctor with a proposition that I felt would be mutually beneficial to both of us. I asked him if he would write a note verifying my year of birth as 1923. Any apprehensiveness on his part was quickly subsided by my offer of payment. I left there with the note for the C.C.C. and the doctor left with a half-pint of whiskey. He was satisfied, needless to say, and so was I.

I took the note from the doctor and gave it to the officials at the C.C.C. They were satisfied and enlisted me in the camp. I enlisted for a one-year hitch. There was a camp located in Mt. Vernon, only a few miles north of Pittsburg, but I was sent to the camp in Ontario, Wisconsin. It was in the northern part of the state of Wisconsin and a long way from home.

The C.C.C. Camp was quite an experience. We participated in a wide variety of duties during my stay in the camp in northern

Wisconsin. We were involved in many activities that in some way or another was beneficial to the environment. We spent a lot of time planting trees in the area. We planted many cedar trees along hillsides to ease erosion problems, as the trees would prevent the soil from washing away. We also spent many days fighting forest fires in the area. It was tough and could be potentially dangerous, but it was pretty satisfying knowing that what we were doing was very beneficial and helping others.

The camp was in some ways very much like a junior army camp. We participated in drills to help us learn to follow orders in an army type setting. We participated in many drills to help get us into very good physical condition. We worked on cleaning our barracks and our uniforms. We worked on living together in an army type environment. It turned out to be very beneficial to me in a short time period.

After my one-year term was up, I decided not to re-enlist for another year. My dad had gotten a job as a prison guard up north. It was the only real job outside of the home that I knew of him having in all the years that I knew him. He sent word to me of a job that he could get for me there. I took the job.

Not long after I took the job, my father quit and headed back home to Pittsburg. He said he had heard that the government was going to put a moratorium on the changing of jobs. There were rumors going around that the government was going to freeze workers in the jobs that they currently held through the war. Although this was the information that we were hearing, I'm not sure if that's the reason why my father actually quit. He wasn't used to actually working for someone else. He was used to being his own boss while operating his still at home. The job at the prison was a pretty good job, but for him I imagine it was quite an adjustment.

I kept my job for several months. I didn't mind it too bad. There were definitely worse ways to make a living. I used to send half of my paycheck home to Pittsburg to help with the family's expenses. My father had treated me with a great deal more respect after I had returned from the C.C.C. Camp and we were now on a little better terms. I was grateful to him for helping me get the job at the prison in Northern Illinois. I probably wouldn't have had any paycheck at all if it weren't for him, so I was more than happy to help the family. I guess I still found myself trying to take care of my mom.

I continued to work in Northern Illinois until the imminent onset of an event, which would be the most life-changing event in my life and also in many other lives in our country.

Chapter 7

In the late 1930's and into the early 1940's we, in Southern Illinois continued to hear about the war that was breaking out over seas. We listened to reports about how Nazi Germany had rolled through Europe and was playing dominoes with border countries. We heard about this Hitler fellow, who was a tyrant dictator who was bent on world domination. In late 1941 he was well on his way to accomplishing that feat. France was already under Nazi rule and Great Britain was beginning to bend under the repeated pressure of the continual bombing threat by Germany.

Rumors were flying around the area as to if and when the United States would become involved in the warfare. Many people thought we should just ignore what was going on in Europe and mind our own business. We were only a few years removed from World War I, and many Americans knew the devastation of war and were reluctant to get involved in the fighting.

There were also many "warhawks" who thought that we should not only get involved, but thought that we should have become involved in the war many months earlier. They believed that if we sat back and let Hitler have his rein, that when he was done with his conquering of Europe that he would then set his sights on the United States. This was the nature of the talk and debate going on in our area in late 1941.

It seemed like any other Sunday morning. It was very early in the Southern Illinois winter. It was early December and the environment was preparing for the onset of the long winter months. This particular Sunday morning would be vastly different than any other people and I had lived through before.

Many people in the area attended church on Sunday morning. This was a common practice for most people in our area. Our family, however, had never become involved in attending a church in the area. I'm not sure exactly why, but we never attended. I would change this drastic omission later in my life, as I realized my need to worship God.

There was an elderly man in the area named Mr. Arnold. He was a nice man who lived in our neighborhood. He was a regular attendee of worship services on Sunday mornings. As he was up and getting ready for service on this Sunday morning, he happened to have his radio on. His radio ran on batteries and this was something that most people in the area didn't have.

Early on that morning of Sunday, December 7, 1941, while he was listening in, the radio station interrupted its regular broadcast for an announcement from President Franklin Delano Roosevelt. President Roosevelt announced to the citizens of the United States of America that Japan had bombed our naval base located in Hawaii. We would learn later that the attack was much more devastating even than first believed. Many men were killed and our fleet in the Southwest Pacific was dealt a crushing blow by the surprise attack.

The President announced that we were declaring war on the Empire of Japan. By agreement, this would also mean that we would be in effect declaring war on all the Axis countries as well, since they would declare war on us. The rumors of war had given way to actual battle. It was something that almost everyone seemed to believe was inevitable. There would be no more talk about whether we should become involved in the war, or not. Japan had put an end to the debate. We were now officially at war.

Mr. Arnold went about spreading the sad news throughout the neighborhood. As I heard the word of the attack, I didn't realize at that moment how important that that day would be to me personally.

The people in town were in a frenzy about the news of the surprise attack on Pearl Harbor. Most people had never heard of Pearl Harbor before the news of the attack by the Japanese. I had no idea where it was before the news. I later learned that it was located in Hawaii. It evidently was one of our more strategically placed bases in the Southwest Pacific. It was now crippled from the devastating beating it took.

There was some talk that seemed to criticize our forces for not being ready for the attack. Some people thought that the President should have made sure we were ready for a possible attack. I guess it was another case of hindsight being twenty-twenty, only in this case it cost many men their lives and our country took a devastating hit that it would have to recover from very quickly.

Most of the conversation centered on the Japanese. I think one word would describe the feelings of most people in the area and probably around the entire country – outrage! The country of Japan had seemingly gone from a forethought in most people's minds, to the focus of the boiling rage of an entire nation. The people were venting the frustration and fear that they felt onto the Japanese.

I later would hear many incredible stories of the cruelty that was inflicted on Japanese Americans after Pearl Harbor. Many of these Americans of Japanese origin had been born and raised in the United States and probably most of them were just as outraged at the Japanese government as the rest of us.

I guess the treatment of the Japanese was especially brutal on the West Coast. There were probably many reasons for this fact. First of all there were many more Japanese Americans on the West Coast than other parts of the country. Also, there was the proximity of the Western United States to Japan and Pearl Harbor. There evidently were many rumors flying around the West Coast about a possible Japanese strike somewhere along the California coastline. People were still concentrating on the attack at Pearl Harbor. Many felt that if the Japanese could land a surprise blow to our forces in Hawaii that they might try the same thing with the United States mainland.

Some dispelled this notion saying that while the Japanese could hit Pearl Harbor, they didn't have bombers that could make it the distance to the California coast. This was the fodder of many debates after Pearl Harbor.

The Japanese Americans were also looked at with much suspicion at this time. There were also rumors abounding that the Japanese had sent in spies to help set up an attack on California. Because of these suspicions our country was guilty of one of the most incredible over-reactions in the history of our great country.

In response to the frenzy on the coast, our government decided to try to make sure that they took care of any possible spying problems on the part of the Japanese. Our country set up camps and rounded up many if not most of the Americans of Japanese origin. These people were forced to leave their homes and were housed at these camps. There were cases of these people having their belongings confiscated if there was any kind of behavior that seemed particularly suspicious. Most of these people were just as loyal as any other American citizen. The government seemed to label all Japanese Americans as a possible threat to security.

I imagine that the officials that made the decision to intern the Japanese Americans had good intentions. As in other sad cases in our county's history, it was another classic case of stereotyping an entire race of people for the actions of a few. It heightened and fueled bigotry and discrimination toward all Japanese Americans. Looking back now, it is a sad part of our country's history. Hopefully we learned a lesson from this horrible overreaction by our nation.

A few years later we would witness a frighteningly similar event in Europe regarding the Jews. It's very scary to think of how close our county's behavior was to the Nazis. Granted we didn't physically exterminate anyone, but we certainly were guilty of a horrible act toward innocent people.

Many men in the area responded to the attack on Pearl Harbor by enlisting in the armed forces. Most seemed primed and ready to get revenge on the Japanese for their actions. My father had served in World War I and was beyond the age that the government was targeting for service. The first person in our family to enlist was dad's brother. I remember dad relating many horrible stories of battle from his days in World War I as he gave his brother a ride to sign up. I didn't see my father get too emotional very often, unless you count anger, usually at me. On this day, though, he was very emotional. As he said goodbye to his brother, he cried at the thought of him going into battle. It was a side of my dad that I was not witness to very often. It was another instance in which I knew that my dad was definitely not all bad.

Like many other men at the time I wanted to enlist, but I was too young. I was actually only fifteen at the time of the attack on Pearl Harbor. I did, however, have a document that stated that I was two years older than that. That meant that though I really was only ready to turn sixteen on my birthday in February, officially I was about to turn eighteen. This would make me old enough to enlist. I finally got the opportunity to enlist on June 10, 1942, at the tender age of just over sixteen years, though according to the Army I was eighteen.

As the days neared to my time of departure, nothing much was mentioned about me leaving home. Nobody seemed to care too much about the fact that I would be departing to risk my life to take part in battle.

On the morning of June 10th, I had to rise very early in the morning to head out. I got up and was ready to depart at about 5 a.m. Everyone else stayed in bed, not even getting up to see me off. I didn't expect a big send-off, but you would have thought that my parents would want to at least say good-bye to me. You would think they would at least want to do that with me going off to war, maybe never to return again. It's hard for me to believe, but they didn't even get up.

The only one in the family to bother to get out of bed to see me off was my youngest brother, Jack. He was very upset about my leaving. He grabbed me by the leg and pleaded with me not to go away and leave him. He always had been close to me. I was sorry that he was upset, but I have to admit that it felt good to think that at least he seemed to care about me. I then left my home not knowing whether I would ever see it or my family sleeping soundly in it again.

As I started the walk to meet Paul Matthews, who owned the truck that was going to take me and the others in the area that had enlisted to catch the train to Chicago, many things went through my mind. I couldn't help but think about my family's reaction to my departure, or maybe I should say lack of reaction. I appreciated the fact that Jack had showed his concern for my leaving, but it's hard to describe the feeling that I had at the thought of my parents staying in bed. I just could never imagine having a child that was about to go off to war and not even acknowledge it. After all these years I still can't imagine it.

As I got closer to town and the truck that I would make the trip to Marion in, I started to see a bit of a crowd gather. There were about twenty-five people or so milling around the Matthews pick-up truck. I reasoned that they were there to see off the other boys.

All of a sudden I found myself having my hand shaken, being hugged, and actually kissed by several of the crowd. They were not only there to see off the other boys, they were there to say good-bye to me also. I couldn't believe it. Many of my neighbors wished me well, or said they'd be praying for my safe return. I also received numerous well wishes from people I barely knew, or didn't know at all. They didn't care whether they knew me personally or not. They were just there to show their support to a group of men going off to defend their country. I sometimes still get chills as I think of this outpouring of support.

There were seven of us boys who crawled into the back of that truck for the trip to the train. As we sat there in the truck as we started our journey to Marion, every last one of us shed many tears at the thought of the gesture of the townspeople. It was a very emotional time for seven farm boys heading out into who knows what.

We finally made it to Marion and the train. We said our thanks and good-byes to Paul Matthews and then boarded the train to Chicago. I had ridden several trains over the last few years, but this was the first in which I was a legitimate passenger. I wondered if there were any passengers that were not legitimate. Although the hobos mainly jumped freight trains, I still figured there just might be a few passengers that the train's officials knew nothing about.

Not only was I really too young to join up, I also wasn't very big. Our family didn't starve, but we never had an abundance of food either. Actually sometimes we were pretty close to starving. Remember Kentucky? Anyway, because of this, I definitely wasn't carrying around any extra weight. I learned on the train trip that this could be a problem for me.

I hadn't realized up to that point that there was a minimum weight to be able to enlist. The minimum weight was 121 pounds. I know that that miniscule weight doesn't sound like much of a problem, but to me it was a big problem. I didn't get the chance to weigh myself much, but I knew from the other boys and their weights that I was definitely gonna be close.

Some people might have thought that this was my chance. This was my opportunity to get out of service. In the last several years with Vietnam and such it has been well reported of different ways that a young man could disqualify himself from service. Not reaching the minimum weight could be my excuse. It would be a legitimate reason to get to go back home.

The problem was that I didn't want a reason to be disqualified from service. I didn't want to go back home. Even though it would seem to be a legitimate reason to avoid enlistment, it was not what I wanted. I would have been ashamed to be rejected. I would have been ashamed to go home. I really wanted to serve. I wanted to fight for my country. It may go against the thinking of many today, but it meant something to me. I considered it an honor to be able to respond to the call of my country at a critical time for our nation.

I knew that I might very well not make the required weight of 121 pounds. I had to do something. I had to find something to eat and quick. I ran onto some bananas. I ate and ate and ate some more. I was afraid that I might have defeated my purpose by eating too much and getting sick, but I managed to keep them down. I ate bananas the entire trip to Chicago.

It managed to pay off though. When we got to Chicago, one of the first things that they check is your weight. I held my breath as they checked the scale. I knew it would be close. It was, but luckily I was just over the minimum weight of 121 pounds. Without the bananas on the trip, I probably would have been sent back home to my Southern Illinois home.

After going through the physical and check in at Chicago, I was sent to basic training in Arkansas. I was headed to Camp Chaffee. It was there that the army would assume the task of trying to teach me to be a soldier. I had an advantage over many of the other young men in our group since I had spent some time in the C.C.C. Camp in Wisconsin. There I had learned many things that I would go through again in Camp Chaffee during basic training.

During my stay at Camp Chaffee the weather was brutally hot during the day, but rather cool at night. We spent the day going through many of the same drills and such that I had been through at the C.C.C. camp in Wisconsin. We did drills to improve our physical condition for combat. We went through the importance of following orders of superior officers on the battlefield. We were exposed to the use of the types of weapons that we would carry in battle. They tried to hone our shooting abilities and school us in the maneuvers important in hand to hand combat. I paid pretty close attention since I was smart enough to realize that at some point my life might depend on my knowledge of these things. Later on, it would.

We went through some types of maneuvers in the swamp area down in Louisiana. It was here in which my basic training would take a dangerous turn.

The group was in the midst of performing a drill that called for each of us to climb the side of a huge rock. I was in the middle of my ascent up the side when I ran into an unexpected obstacle.

We had been warned about some of the wildlife that was indigenous to the swamplands of Louisiana. One of these critters was the rattlesnake. These could be particularly dangerous not only because of their poisonous venom, but also because they were sometimes very difficult to see. This was especially true in the cliffs we were climbing. The jagged ledges gave the snakes a good place to seek cover from the daytime sunshine. One had to keep a sharp ear out because the best way to not be surprised by the rattlers was to hear their notorious rattler.

I was in the middle of the drill. I was making my way up the side of the rock, as were the others in our group. That's when I heard it! I heard the sound of a vigorously shaking rattle. I started to get a sick feeling as it sunk it what I would soon be dealing with.

I followed the sound straight to the spot on the ledge directly in front of me where a large rattlesnake sat nestled and ready to strike. I immediately froze as I looked eye to eye at the rattler. I knew that if the rattler detected the slightest movement that it would undoubtedly strike. It would have been bad enough to be faced with the frightening task of staring down an extremely poisonous rattlesnake, but I also was dangling on the side of the cliff. It was not the most promising of positions to find ones self in.

As fiercely as I tried to hold on and not make a move, I felt my left hand slipping slightly. My hand finally slipped enough for the snake to detect it. The rattler then struck. It bit me on the left wrist. I later leaned that my hand slipping may have saved my life, since the rattler would probably have bitten me right between the eyes had it not sensed my hand movement. A bite there would most likely have been lethal. After the snake bit me, I slid down the side of the rock. I bounced off the side of the ledge and tumbled to the ground.

I don't really remember too much about what happened for the next few moments. I had just been bitten by a poisonous rattlesnake and then proceeded to fall of a high ledge and land on the ground below. All I really remember is feeling incredibly dizzy. Needless to say, I was not in good shape.

The medics quickly attended to me. They rushed onto the scene of my accident. Not only did I need treatment for the rattlesnake bite, but I also was pretty banged up. They quickly sucked out the deadly poison. They gave me a serum to deal with the poison in my system and attended to my injuries from the fall. The quick response of the medical team paid off.

Since they got to me so quickly and got the poison out of my system, the serum was able to work effectively to curtail the effects of the poison. Evidently at that time many victims of these snakebites would have long term complications from the poison, if they survived at all. I had none of these.

I also was very fortunate not to have broken any bones or be severely hurt by my fall. It was definitely not a pleasant experience, but like many things in my life, it could have been much worse.

Chapter 8

I eventually recovered from my run in with that rattlesnake at Camp Chaffee. It set me back a little in finishing my basic training after spending about thirty-one days recovering, but as I said, I had no lasting effects from the injury. I ended up spending more than a year in Arkansas going through basic. After I finished my training, I was sent east for my trip overseas.

I was sent to Camp Kilmer in New Jersey. There, I was to board a ship that would transfer me and many other fresh recruits to Europe. It was now early spring of 1944, and the United States had been in action in the European theatre for more than two years. We would provide a fresh group of soldiers to support what in many cases were battle weary men.

It was my first trip out to the East Coast. I had traveled extensively now through the Midwest and with basic also through some of the Southeast, but this was my first trip to the Atlantic Coast. It was nice to see a different part of the country. I would, however, have preferred to have made the trip under more pleasant circumstances.

After arriving at Camp Kilmer, we were scheduled to board the Queen Mary for the trip to South Hampton, England. When I first got a glimpse of the Queen Mary I was absolutely awestruck. It was huge. I believe someone told me in was bigger than the size of three football fields. I had never seen anything so big. I just kept thinking about how in the world something that big could actually float. I wasn't sure if I wanted to get on it, or not. I don't remember anyone giving me much of a choice in the matter. I got on board with the others and we set off for Great Britain.

We were warned before we got on board the massive ocean liner that it would be a new experience for us. Our superiors told us that it might take us a few days for us to get our sea legs under us. They said it was not uncommon for young men to spend the first few days of the trip leaning over the side of the ship and emptying his stomach's contents into the ocean. It was not a very pleasant thought.

I saw many men get sick, but it didn't seem to have too much effect on me. Today, I guess they have Dramamine and such to help alleviate the seasickness caused by the ocean's massive waves, but most men were forced to just tough it out. They did, but I'm sure it was not a very peasant experience to live through.

There were twelve ships that made up our convoy on our trip to England. It was quite a site to look out and see that many ships cutting through the Atlantic en route to Europe. It made me realize how massive the undertaking of our participation in World War II actually was. It made me feel very patriotic just to get the opportunity to be even a small part of it.

As we made our voyage across the Atlantic Ocean I mostly performed guard duty. It was mine and several other men's responsibility to stand guard on the bridge of the huge ship. We were charged with the task of scanning the waters of the Atlantic for the enemy. We were to watch for enemy ships, submarines, or planes. We were also supposed to keep a close eye out for dead bodies floating on the water. This could be a sign of something happening in the area. If any of us recruits saw any of these things we were to report it to the Captain of the ship immediately giving him the details and location of the sighting over the P.A. system. One morning during our journey, I managed to spot something during my duty.

It was very early one morning during our journey and I was stationed on my post for morning guard duty. All of the other ships in our convoy had left us because they were expecting a fuel tanker to come to refuel ships. Because of this there were no other visible ships in the immediate area. I continued my duty for a while that morning until I noticed something odd.

I looked over the horizon and saw four submarines coming toward us. I was frantic with the ominous sight across the sea. I quickly responded by notifying the Captain of the ship. While I went about the process of letting the Captain in on the sight, many others noticed the excitement and found out about my sighting. We almost had a panic situation on our hands.

This situation we were in was extremely frightening for several reasons. We were out in the middle of the Atlantic Ocean without any defense from enemy subs. We were not equipped to handle an enemy onslaught. With the departure of the other ships in our convoy, we had no immediate help. Our ship and the hundreds of passengers would be sitting ducks for these enemy subs. It was an incredibly helpless feeling that I felt at that moment.

When the ones of us who saw the subs calmed down enough to listen, we found out that the subs were actually Americans. They were ours! The subs were heading in to be refueled by the tankers that would be aiding the rest of the ships in the convoy. It was a false alarm. It had caused a great deal of panic, but it was for naught, luckily. What a relief for me and the others who had just about given our ship up for target practice for a Nazi submarine!

I learned a lesson from the false alarm. It would be the first, if you don't count the rattlesnake, of many instances during my wartime service in which I would be faced with a frightening situation. I learned that there was a correct way to deal with an apparent life-threatening situation, and an incorrect way to deal with a life-threatening situation. I now realized that one of the most important things to make sure you do, if not the most important, is to keep your cool. There was no way for anyone to deal effectively with a crucial situation if they panicked. It could mean the difference in life and death for an individual or even a whole platoon. I would learn because of that incident how important this could be in battle. I would go on to use this to my advantage many times during my next few months in Europe.

The trip to South Hampton, England took all of 21 days. In some ways it seemed like more. As I mentioned, I didn't get seasick during the trip, but I have to admit it sure was good to see land after three weeks at sea.

During our stay in South Hampton, we were housed in old barracks that were left over from World War I. We stayed in England for two weeks. We were awaiting orders as to our next course of action. We knew we would be sent into battle soon. It was odd that they waited so long to send us anywhere. I would have thought that there were probably many areas where battles were raging in which we could have been a great help during that time period that we waited in England. I didn't know the plan that they had in store for us.

The time we spent in England seemed to drag on. Time seemed to pass by very slowly for all of us as we waited there. We were all starting to get very anxious about where our unit would be going. As the days passed and we continued to remain in South Hampton, rumors started to fly around the base. Word was going around that something was up. We were hearing that we were not just going to be sent into some battle that was already going on to assist our troops.

We started to hear that we were going to be part of something special, something very special. We were.

We had all heard rumors, even in basic training, about the talk of an impending invasion of France. We knew it would eventually come, what we didn't know was when and where. We would soon find the answers to both of these questions.

We later leaned that during this time the Allied leaders were busily planning strategy. They were in the midst of putting the finishing touches on our next course of action. While we were heading to and then waiting in England, President Roosevelt had been meeting in conferences in Quebec with English Prime Minister Winston Churchill and in Tehran with both Churchill and Soviet leader Joseph Stalin.

This was, to say the least a meeting of "strange bed fellows". While the United States and Great Britain had formed a very solid and long-lasting allied relationship long before the war had broken out, this was not the case with the Soviet Union. The union among the three countries had come about not by a similar ruling governmental ideology, because the USSR and Stalin's dictatorship in a communism form of government flew in the face of everything the United States and also Great Britain stood for. The three countries did, however, have one major thing in common in the middle of 1944 – a common enemy. That common enemy was one German dictator by the name of Adolph Hitler.

Needless to say there was not a great deal of trust in the most precarious union between the United States and England with the Soviet Union. Just a few months earlier the Soviets had been on the other side of the table.

Stalin had signed a pact with Hitler only to have the German leader turn on the Soviets and attack them. Germany had moved well into Soviet territory and was not beyond reach of completely overrunning their former ally. Stalin's contempt and distrust for Roosevelt and Churchill were surpassed only by his need for revenge against his now hated German counterpart. While these things played out among our leaders, we waited.

Our unit, which was the 24th Cavalry Unit, was finally given orders. We were to make our way across the English Channel and secure an island off the coast of France. Our superiors told us that the Germans inhabited the island and that they were entrenched there with heavy artillery. It would be my first taste of actual combat during the war.

On June 4, 1944, our unit assembled at South Hampton for our departure. I was very nervous, but I have to say that it actually felt pretty good to finally know what we were going to be doing. We then were served with another indication that this was going to be something special. One major indication of the importance of the operation that we were going to take part in was the way we were given a special send off. General Dwight D. Eisenhower greeted us.

General Eisenhower spoke to our unit and gave us a very motivational send off. It would not be the last time that I had an encounter with the General who would later serve as President of the United States. Less than a year later we would meet under different circumstances. After the General finished speaking, we were then loaded onto very large pontoon boats for our trip across the English Channel toward the island.

I don't know what the other members of the unit were thinking at this time, but I knew that they didn't send General Eisenhower just anywhere. He would not have been here had this not been a pivotal operation. It would later prove to be just that.

When our unit made it to the island, we found no Germans. We found no one. The island, much to our surprise was uninhabited. The rumors of the Germans being there were just that, rumors. We proceeded to secure the island, which was just off the French Coast. We didn't have to be rocket scientists to be able to figure out where we were headed next.

We stayed on the island for two days. We were waiting for other forces to cross the English Channel and join us in a massive invasion of France. We knew it would be a terrible battle.

While word of the Germans being entrenched on the island was just rumor, we knew that the Germans were definitely entrenched on the coasts of France. They had had more than six months to set up there and establish themselves on the beaches. Any attempt at liberating France would be very costly.

During conversations with some members of the unit, I found that they had many questions running through their mind, as did I. We found ourselves wondering if the Germans were better than we were. Were they better prepared? Were they better fighters? Did they have better equipment than we did? We pondered these questions in our minds.

Remember you were talking about mainly farm boys from the United States. Even though we had been well trained for battle, when it came down to it we were mostly just kids who had never lifted a rifle to anything other than a tin can, or maybe an animal we were stalking for food. We had heard for months about the battles raging across Europe and we knew that the Germans would be more experienced if for no other reason than the fact that they had been involved in the war for a longer period of time.

We all also knew many men would die, even if things went as planned during the invasion. This fact was what was weighing very heavily on our minds as we waited on the island for the impending battle that was to take place the next day.

Chapter 9

Adolph Hitler had expected an Allied attempt at the liberation of France. He expected the Allies to attempt a landing in Northwest Europe sometime in the spring of 1944. It later became common knowledge that Hitler actually welcomed the Allies arrival. The German Dictator believed that this was his chance to actually win the war. He believed that if his German forces could repel an attempted landing, that the Allied forces would not shortly try it again. He believed that this would allow the German army to focus on the eastern front and the Soviets. This would let him move more men onto the Russian front for a last push toward Moscow.

The Germans were anticipating the siege to come at or near Calais on the northern coast of France. This was, in fact, the most logical choice. It was the shortest water route for the Allied forces to take. It was a short distance from Great Britain where the Allies could prepare for an invasion; at least this was what the Germans believed.

Unbeknownst to the German Dictator was the fact that a British intelligence operation was in the works. The operation, tabbed Ultra had broken codes in some key German transmissions. They had learned specifically where the Germans had been anticipating a landing in France.

This ended up being a crucial piece of intelligence work. Knowing the thoughts of their German counterparts, the Allies stationed a "phantom army" in Kent, which because of its location would only heighten the German's belief that the landing would come from the north. All these things were going on behind the scenes as we prepared for our trip.

The landing was actually scheduled for an earlier launch, but had to be postponed. We heard there were delays in getting some of the necessary equipment needed to undertake the massive attack. There were also some problems with the weather in Northern France. Our superiors wanted the weather conditions to be the most favorable possible. There also had been some tidal conditions that had to be just right. These problems eventually cleared and we were given the go-ahead for the operation.

We were loaded onto the pontoon boats for our trip across the water to our destination. We were headed for the French Coast and a massive attempt at liberating the country of France. Our unit was loaded into the pontoon boats like sardines for the impending trip.

After we left the island and headed across the English Channel, we met up with many more of our invading forces. We joined them for the trip to France and what at that time would be the most massive amphibious invasion in history.

That's when I started to look into the eyes of the other men on our boat. I saw many different looks in the eyes of the men. Some of them showed their concern very vividly. You could see the fear and anxiety in their eyes. Some of the men tried to play down the situation. They either were very brave or very good at masking their fears.

I thought about many things as we made our way to my first battle. I wondered if I would make it back. I knew that as I looked across the boat that many of the men I saw headed into France would never make it out of there. They would never see home or their families again. I wondered if I would be one of the fortunate ones that would make it through this day.

I could never describe vividly enough what would happen in the next several hours. I have read many books, and articles about this day, and while many were very well written, none of them actually described the moments of that day as well as I picture them in my mind.

I've watched many movies and television shows or documentaries covering this event, but there is just something missing. As I made the decision to try to convey my life on paper, I tried and tried to rectify this. I tried to describe the day that would prove to be the longest day of my life accurately.

I wanted to use all the right words, all the most appropriate adjectives to describe to prospective readers what many others and I went through on that day. I went through them all. I exhausted all the listings in just about every known thesaurus. I scanned dictionary after dictionary to find just the right definitions to help correctly portray what occurred.

Then it hit me. I realized that it just couldn't be done. There is no way I can describe that day to suit me. Many much more talented people than me have tried. Now don't get me wrong. I'm not in any way, shape, or form criticizing those men and women who have written about this battle. Most all accounts that I have read and those that I have witnessed on screen have been very well done. My point is that if you actually lived through it, if you actually were there on the beaches of Normandy, there is no way to relate it to people in any form of media in a fashion that actually lives up to the day itself.

I guess it's similar to a reader who has read a novel and then goes to the movies to see the novel portrayed on film. Many times the film doesn't do the book justice. The reader has pictured the characters, setting, and scenes in their mind and the actors or directors don't have the same vision. It's a very common experience for those who read material that ends up on screen. Describing the actions and events of June 6, 1944 is very much like this scenario.

I hope you readers never do quite get the completely accurate portrayal of that day I'm about to relate to you because the only way for you to get this picture is to live through it and I pray that you never do.

Operation Overlord – or as it was later referred to D-Day was now underway. It was an absolutely incredible sight. The English Channel was covered with Allied ships each filled with troops ready to land on the beaches of Normandy.

Approximately somewhere between 6:30 and 7:30 a.m. I unloaded from my craft and headed along with thousands of other men toward the coastline. The allies would make landings on five beaches including Gold, Juno, Omaha, Sword, and the beach that our unit infiltrated, Utah Beach.

Our general in command of our unit was General Theodore Roosevelt Jr. He was the son of one-time president, Theodore "Teddy" Roosevelt and also a cousin of the current president, Franklin D. Roosevelt. I think that the General was just there as a symbolic gesture, as would be the case with most generals in this situation. At this time, the General was well along in years and I believe probably wanted to be part of the operation. He showed leadership to the men by standing on the beach and yelling orders out to the oncoming troops.

Shortly after D-Day, General Roosevelt was sent back to the United States. A few weeks later I believe he had a heart attack and passed away.

As I embarked on Utah Beach and tried to make my way inland, men were falling from fatal wounds all around me. The beaches as we were warned were heavily mined and fortified. The Germans were set up in what we referred to as "pill boxes". These were small concrete bunkers that the Germans had set up to put men in to repel our attack. The German troops would sit in the concrete barriers and fire their weapons out of a small hole. It made it very difficult for our artillery to penetrate their defenses.

After having built up one of the largest and most powerful invasion forces in history, we continued our assault. The Germans had set up a stronghold and it would be very difficult to establish ourselves on the beaches. Men continued to fall on all sides of me. With all the artillery going off and the gunfire, it looked like the fourth of July back home.

I made it to an area that had more cover. How I or any of the others made it there is absolutely amazing. It was just a matter of the other men and me that made it, being lucky, at least that's what I thought at the time. I later realized that there was definitely much more than luck involved in my ultimate survival. I saw some of the men fall whose fate I had wondered about on our trip across the English Channel. One moment they were alive and the next they were gone. I would have been incredibly sad, but I didn't have time to be sad at the moment.

As difficult as it seemed to be, there were some circumstances that were aiding our mission. For the last two months the Allies had been unleashing a barrage of bombing raids on France. They had concentrated their attacks on key points such as, railroads, bridges, airfields, and other crucial facilities to transportation and communication.

Our fleet of naval ships was there to do more than serve as transportation for service men. As we made our way inland, the heavy artillery guns on our naval vessels pounded the Germans trying to repel our attack.

Paratroopers had also been dropped behind German defense lines. They were scheduled to help sever communications and try to seize key posts. They did their job and did it very effectively.

It was a very bloody and costly battle for us, but by the end of the day, despite an extremely fierce German resistance, we had secured all five of the beaches of Normandy. The invasion which was located on the Northern French coast and included the beach front between Cherbourg and Le Havre included participation of more than 150,000 allied troops. There were about 5,000 ships involved on the waters off the coast and around 11,000 aircraft supporting the invasion.

There was still much work to do, but the Allies had gone a long way on this day, June 6, 1944, D-Day, to ending Adolph Hitler's attempt at world dominance. Many lives were lost, but what a way to be forced to sacrifice it all. What a worthy cause! The families of the men who died on that day should feel a measure of pride that their loved one not only stood for something, but also died for something. Without their sacrifice, the world would undoubtedly be a much different place today.

Chapter 10

After the successful landing we had made on D-Day, the Allies were now firmly established on the beaches of France. Though many will attest to the fact that Adolph Hitler was a brilliant strategist on battle, the infamous German dictator had made a crucial tactical mistake by refusing to believe that the Normandy landing was in fact the actual point of invasion by the Allies. He had refused to free up other German soldiers stationed in other more likely locations for the invasion. Because of this the Germans at Normandy did not have the luxury of any extra forces being sent to help repel the Allied landing on the beaches at Normandy.

Though the indescribably crucial landing was a success, it was not, however, the end of the war. There would be many significant battles yet to be fought. The Germans had not been able to repel our landing, but they by no means had given up. They continued to fight fiercely. We were able to widen the area that we had taken control of along the beach. We were successful at broadening our forces, but we had not been successful at extended our invading forces into the boundaries of France.

While we continued to widen our seized area along the beach, the Germans had many serious troubles on their other fronts. In mid to late June, the Soviet armies had mounted a counter offensive on the eastern front. After many months of retreat and losses at the hands of the Germans, the Soviets had regrouped and were now on the offensive. After many successes in battles, there was a much-celebrated Soviet march of German prisoners through the streets of downtown Moscow. There was much satisfaction on the Soviets side after being brutalized by the Nazis for several months in battle after battle.

As the Third Reich began to unravel, Hitler would be faced with more adversity. This time the adversity would come from within. On July 20, 1944, there was an assassination attempt on the German leader's life. The bomb involved in the attempt on Hitler's life actually did explode that day. The blast wounded a number of officers. Some of those men among Hitler's officers were killed. Hitler escaped with only minor injuries.

It was easy to see that the attempted assassination was an inside job. There was much speculation as to who had been involved in the foiled attempt. Rommel was a suspect, but before there were any definitive answers, he committed suicide.

As Hitler was dealing with troubles from within, his troops were still fighting fiercely to hold their positions near the French coast. We were stalled near the coast as we tried to break through the German lines and extend into France.

While we were in France, I suffered my first two battle wounds. Neither was of the classic kind. The first happened when I was a jeep driver on night reconnaissance just before we reached the hedgerow country. I was with another troop in my jeep and we had encountered a German tank shooting 88mm shells at us. These large shells were usually used on tanks and large artillery, not people. We escaped the tank, but not before we ran into a barbed wire fence and hit a ditch. I was literally cut to pieces and suffered a broken nose though I was fortunate to be alive.

The other incident happened in the hedgerow country of France. I was out scouting around for food or drink. I came upon a farmhouse and noticed a cellar where many times wine was stored. I heard something moving and decided to get out of there. I was slightly too late. A German appeared with what we used to call a "burp gun". It was named this because of the sound it made. It was made to shoot from short range and had only a minimal effect at a distance. The German chased me over and sometimes through hedgerows. I got hit several times, but the shells didn't penetrate. I outran the German and made it back to our lines where my buddies cut him down quickly. After I was safe I examined myself and found some 10 to 15 shells in my back and butt. Even after all these years I don't do too much talking about those wounds. I guess you can understand why. It seems awfully funny now, but it sure didn't as I was literally running for my life.

After D-Day and all that surrounded it, I almost felt myself not taking the dangers of war very seriously. As I look back now at my attitude during this time, it's still difficult for me to believe those were my feeling at the time. I never found myself very worried about the life-threatening situation we were constantly faced with.

Most of the other members of my unit were very nervous and completely on edge, as they should have been. As was the case in

England, it was tough waiting, not knowing what we would do next. I did my best to try to alleviate this problem.

I would do my best to lighten the mood as we went through this difficult situation. I would tell jokes and just act silly in general. I used to sometimes sing songs and do my best to try to entertain the other troops. It was my way of helping deal with the situation that we were in.

I started feeling proud that I could do something to help our unit even in some small way. I guess I was probably the only member of our unit that could have played the part of entertainer/comedian. All the others were just too keyed up to act silly like me. I became pretty renowned for my antics. In fact I developed quite a reputation among the members of my unit.

I recall one particular incident regarding this issue. Our unit had made it to an area referred to as the communication trenches in France. It consisted of many trenches that had been dug around the French countryside during World War I for protection against the enemy.

During our time in France we used the trenches for the same protection against the enemy as our World War I counterparts. Our unit was pinned down and could not make our way out of the trenches. We needed help from reinforcements from another unit. Everyone was extremely nervous. Chances of our unit's survival didn't seem particularly good.

As I waited in a trench for our help to possibly come, I got a message. Word had been passed back from a trench about five hundred yards ahead for me to come up to the front. As I said earlier, I wasn't as tense, or nervous as most of the others in the unit, but this made me a little nervous. I couldn't imagine what in the world they wanted from me. Were they going to send me out on some mission to try to help get us out of this situation we were in? I didn't know what it would be, but I knew that whatever the order would be, it had to be extremely dangerous. I thought about all the possibilities as I made my way up to the front.

When I finally made it to the trenches on the front lines, I was surprised to hear of my proposed assignment. The men in the trench wanted to be cheered up. They were almost crazed with worry from our desperate situation, and needed someone to help lighten things up before they cracked. I was extremely surprised, but was very relieved to hear of their request.

I proceeded to joke around with the men. I sang a few songs for them. I remember that the men had one particular request for me. They wanted to hear a Roy Acuff song entitled "Way Back in the Hills". They laughed and laughed as I sang this song. The men in the trench were almost exclusively from the north, and they got a big kick out of the song that was popular in the south.

I was really the only "southern boy" in the unit, if you count Southern Illinois as southern. It was southern in comparison to the areas that most of the other men of the unit came from. Many of them were from New York, New Jersey, North Dakota, etc. They liked to hear my accent, which I never knew I had until I met these guys.

I guess all of my antics were some kind of defense mechanism. It was my way of dealing with an extremely difficult situation. I guess the human mind can take only a certain amount of stress and strain before it finds a way to deal with it. Entertainment and humor was the way I dealt with it.

It also made me feel good to be of some help. Making a "nut" out of myself was my way of contributing to the positive morale of our unit. It definitely seemed to help. I got a chance to see men smile and laugh, some of which I had never seen even flash a grin before. It was nice to be able to help make men who had very little reason to be happy at the time, actually feel good, even for just a brief moment. It was what I had become known for in my unit.

I got along well with about every one in my unit especially with my knack for entertaining them during battle. About a week or so after we landed in France on D-Day, I met the person who would become my best friend. Rose and I hit it off right from the start.

My buddy, Rose was a young blond haired kid from California. He was much different than most of the other members of our unit I was acquainted with. A good number of our men were hard nosed, or at least they tried to be. Rose was a very gentle young man. Many of the members of our unit cursed on a regular basis. I never heard Rose do any kind of cursing, even when faced with life-threatening situations. Most of the men drank alcohol, at least they did on the rare chance they got the opportunity to. Rose didn't drink.

Yeah, Rose was different, all right. When I first got to know him, I asked him about his being different than most of the men of our unit. I wondered why his views on life were so vastly different than most. He was very quick to set me straight as to the reason he led a much different way of life. It was Christ. Rose was a Christian.

As I mentioned, my family had never gone to church or anything when I was back home in Southern Illinois. Even though we never went to services ourselves, I used to see many people back in Pittsburg who were Christians. I guess I usually associated Christians with mostly old people who weren't allowed to do anything to have fun.

Rose had a regular routine that he followed. When he would awake, or anytime our unit was faced with some type of particularly difficult situation, Rose prayed. I asked him what he was praying for and he told me that he was praying for all the members of our unit and our safe return.

I'm sure many men had their faith tested in those battle situations that we continued to face day after day. I would imagine that men who had never prayed much in their lives were asking God to let them make it home alive. It was different with Rose. I got the feeling that this was the way Rose lived everyday, not just in these tense war situations we were faced with. I, and I think all the men in our unit, respected Rose and his religious beliefs.

Rose would have a great impact on my life in many ways. Seeing his deep convictions caused me for the first time in my life to really question my belief in God. As I stated, I had no family background of church attendance. I had no reference to fall back on. I found myself paying close attention to Rose and how he lived his life. I used to question him about his beliefs. I never really gave my live to Christ at this time, but through Rose's help, I began to understand the importance of committing my life to something that meant something. Rose had a peace that I was searching for. He had something that I wanted and I began my quest for it.

Rose and I became best of friends. We stuck together very closely and watched each other's backs. I felt safe with him and I believe he felt safe with me, too. I had never really had a close friend back home. When I was small, I never got the chance to play with other kids to develop any close friendships. I was too busy with household chores. When I was an adolescent and teenager I was too busy either taking care of my siblings or my mom to make many friends.

Rose was really my first close friend. He was my best friend. I grew to think the world of my new buddy. It felt pretty good to finally have a trusted, true friend.

In late July of 1944 we finally began a serious breakout toward inland France and away from Normandy. The battles were very fiercely fought and to see the fight left in their soldiers, one would not think that the German army was anywhere near surrendering. It was tough, but it was good to see after being bogged down for more than a month that we were on the move.

Some days we would progress many miles inland and other days we would go only a few feet, if not retreat slightly. The battles continued to be rough. We continued to see men of our unit fall. As each one would not return from a particular battle, I found myself wondering why it had been them and not me.

As our unit continued to fight our way inward, we became more and more familiar with the horrors of battle and maybe more importantly the methods of battle. Each man had a particular responsibility and if that particular assignment was not fulfilled, then it could endanger the entire unit.

One particular assignment that men were definitely not standing in line for was that of scout. The scout would be in charge of making his way ahead of the unit until he actually spotted the enemy. It was the only way for our unit to effectively know the position of the enemy. As you can probably guess, it was a very dangerous duty. The scout was completely without any kind of aid from the unit.

There were specifically two scouts. There was the number one scout and the number two scout. The number one scout was by far the more dangerous of the two. The number one scout was to make his way to actual contact with the enemy. He then would relay the position to the number two scout situated several yards back. The number two scout would then get word back to the unit.

While no one actually wanted the jobs, the accurate performance of these two jobs was crucial for the survival of the entire unit. If the scouts either didn't get word back at all, or were incorrect about enemy position it could mean sending an entire unit into an ambush of some kind.

Our Captain would always ask the unit for volunteers for the two positions. There were usually none. If this was the case, the Captain would then draft someone into the position. I'm not really sure how the Captain did this, but I guess he tried to do it in a fair way.

I'm sure I cannot accurately describe to you the reaction of the two men that were chosen for scout duty, especially the number one scout. As each man was chosen, you could not only see the fear in his eyes, you could actually feel it. It was horrible to say the least.

I remember one particular incident in which the actions of the scouts were critical to our unit's survival. We were making our way into France. As usual, the scouts were off on their prescribed duty. Our unit was heading inland when a German unit without warning of any kind surprised us. The enemy unit appeared from it seemed out of nowhere. It was sudden and deadly. We scrambled to take cover. We tried to go into a makeshift retreat.

As we desperately tried to regroup the unit, it was evident that the scouts had not performed their assignment effectively. They had either mistakenly missed the position of the German unit, or they had been intercepted and were probably lying dead somewhere along the French countryside. Either way, the entire unit was put in harms way and many men were killed.

After the disaster, Rose and I started talking about the scout situation. We talked about the fact that the scouts had not been effective and we barely made it out of there with our lives while many men didn't. We discussed the fear that all the scouts had shown as they were selected for this ominous duty.

I couldn't help but think back to my guard duty on the Queen Mary on the trip over seas. I remembered my false alarm and the panic that was caused by the sighting of the submarines that ended up being ours. I thought about the fact that I realized that I could not do my duty and perform my assigned function if I were panicked, or scared, or at least showed it. I brought that important lesson into my service in France.

We decided that our unit was continually putting our lives in the hands of men who were scared to death. There was no way that they could be effective at the scout position if they were too scared to function correctly. They could not possibly have full use of their faculties in this state. We had almost been wiped out by the surprise German attack. We were not thrilled with the idea of this possibly happening again. We came up with a plan.

Rose and I went to the Captain and volunteered for the positions of scouts. I volunteered for the job as number one scout, while my buddy, Rose, would take the position of number two scout. The Captain expressed his gratitude and I believe he was proud of us for volunteering. We were not thrilled with taking on the dangerous position, but we would rather the safety of the unit be in our hands than in the hands of a soldier who might be too scared to be effective.

Rose and I worked together very well. We made a great team. I would fill the position as number one scout, as Rose took on the number two position. We would go out ahead of the unit, usually several hundred yards in front of our fellow soldiers. When we got a good ways ahead of the unit Rose would set up his position, while I continued on. I had to be very sly to get close to the enemy without being spotted. I would slither my way through weeds and high grass. I would have to crawl around, and sometimes in trees to try to be able to get the best view of the situation.

When I made contact with the enemy I would carefully survey the situation. I would determine the location and position of the enemy. I would try to surmise the German's strength. I would try to calculate the number of troops and units involved. It was up to me to make a recommendation as to what our course of action should be.

I had to decide if it looked like we should initiate contact with the German unit. If it looked like the unit was not at full strength, or was in a vulnerable position I would recommend that we moved ahead. If it looked like there were too many units, or too many men, I would recommend that we avoid contact. We could do this by retreating, by going around the unit, or waiting for back up forces. When the help came we could surround the unit and attack.

When I had something to report then I would get back to a position in which I could see Rose. I would then use hand signals to let him know what I had found out. He would then relay the information back to the unit.

We continued volunteering for the positions and working together. We really started to get it down to a science. It seemed as if we didn't even have to actually signal each other. It almost seemed as if we knew what each other were thinking out there. I really believe that Rose and I got to know each other so well that sometimes we actually did know what the other one was thinking.

There was one other aspect of the routine that was very important to us in the performance of our duty. Before we started out on our assignment each day we paused for prayer. It was really the first prayer that I had ever participated in. It's kind of hard to explain, but even though at the time I didn't really know what my concept of God was, I did know it seemed to make me feel better. It made me feel good to think that there was a higher power looking out for me. I loved to hear Rose's prayer. He was so very sincere in his prayer requests. As time went on, our little prayer time became at least as important to me as it was to Rose.

As we made our way through France, the Allied plans for liberation was taking shape. There had been another landing on French soil. American and French forces had landed on the southern coast. Word was that they were making their way north. If the two fronts could meet, that would spell doom for the Germans.

As Rose and I continued with our duties, I remember one particular day in which I had an odd feeling. Something wasn't quite right. I couldn't put my finger on it, but something was different.

Our unit had made its way to an area in the French countryside. I had been sent out on my usual duty as number one scout and Rose was my back up as number two scout. I left Rose and made my way closer to the area in which we believed that there might be a German unit. As I left Rose I continued to have the same funny feeling I had had earlier.

As I made my way up ahead of Rose, I managed to get several hundred yards ahead of the unit. I came upon a small French village. To this day, I'm not sure of the exact location of the village, but it was somewhere to the south of Paris. It looked like there were only about ten houses in the village. I watched for an extended period of time before I surmised that the village was deserted. I signaled as much to Rose whom then headed back to the unit with the information.

I was extremely cautious as I proceeded through the village. It was a quaint little village, that I probably would have enjoyed visiting under more pleasant circumstances. The original inhabitants of the small settlement had probably fled the Nazis.

I continued to look around the area as I waited for Rose to return with the unit. I examined the homes and the contents in them. It was fascinating to look at the French workmanship in the architecture of the buildings and the items inside as well. It was very interesting to me.

As I looked around though, I continued to have a funny feeling. It was kind of in the pit of my stomach. I wasn't exactly sick, but there was something different. I ignored it, something I would later regret.

I continued to examine the small village. I looked through all but the last house in the village. I entered the small home. It was nice, but very simple. I saw something in this house that was different than the ones I had been through previously. There was some sign of some person or people that had been there in the home and not too far in the past. There were a couple of signs of this. They had given us tips in basic training as to what to look for to decide if there were inhabitants in an area in the recent past.

I felt the stove and it was warm, not hot, but warm. There was some water setting on the stove and it was warm also. There was also a very small fire still smoldering in the stove. These were all signs that someone had been here, and not too long ago. I started to get that feeling again.

I got a little nervous now wondering if someone had been in the village. Actually I didn't really wonder if someone had been in the village in the not too distant past, I knew someone had. What I wondered was who had been there.

There were a few possible scenarios that I reasoned could have happened. If the village were still inhabited by the French, they may have been frightened if they heard or possibly saw our unit in the area. I thought that some Frenchmen who were in hiding from the Germans might have inhabited the village. They could have seen or heard me approaching and left in a hurry.

The next option was not as inviting. A German unit who could be setting a trap for our unit could have inhabited the village. If this were the case, then I needed to get word to Rose and the unit in a hurry.

I quickly decided to get out of the small home to get word back to the unit about the situation that I had discovered in the village. I headed out of the home through the back door. As I started out of the house, I got that sinking feeling again. All I knew was that I wanted to get back to the unit and get there quickly. I wouldn't get that chance.

When I got out of the house I noticed a very ominous sight. There were five Germans there waiting for me, each one of them pointing their weapon directly at my head. Boy, did I have that feeling again. It was the feeling of being captured by the Nazis.

Chapter 11

Helplessness – That's the best word for me to use to describe the situation I had found myself in. I was absolutely totally helpless. It was a terrible feeling. Now I knew what the feeling I was having in the pit of my stomach was as I searched through that village in France. They always say to listen to your instincts. I wish I had done just that. My world had seemingly come to an end.

When I had initially saw the German soldiers waiting for me outside the house, I had kind of a surreal feeling. I just couldn't believe that it was happening. I couldn't believe that I was actually going to be taken prisoner.

The Nazis loaded me into a jeep. I was doing anything I possibly could to slow down this process. I knew that if I could stall for some time it might give Rose enough time to make it back to camp. When Rose gave them the word of the village being deserted, the unit wouldn't waste any time moving forward. They would most likely be encompassing the small French village shortly. I knew I might not survive the battle with the five Germans, but I knew at least that they wouldn't get the satisfaction of taking me as a prisoner of war.

The Germans didn't waste any time. They whisked me into the jeep and we headed out of there before I saw any sign of Rose or our unit. It was true. I was now officially a prisoner of war. I never thought it would happen to me. I never thought I would be captured, but in fact, I had been.

During the ride my mind wondered as I thought about what I was going to face. I had heard all the horror stories of the brutal treatment that our prisoners of war had endured at the hands of the Germans. I heard tales of unspeakable atrocities that our boys had been subject to by the Nazis. I knew that was what I was facing. I remember thinking about these issues, but I can honestly say I don't remember being scared. I guess I didn't have time.

I had kind of an eerie feeling as we made the ride toward the German border. The Germans were conversing among themselves, in German. I, of course, couldn't understand them, but I got the gist of their conversation. They would talk for a moment then look at me and laugh. They were obviously making light of the fact that they had bagged an American. They may have been discussing what they were going to have the opportunity to do once they brought me in. Maybe they were talking about the possible recognition or awards they would receive for successfully capturing an American capitalist. I wasn't sure, but I knew that whatever they were discussing, it didn't bode well for my future.

We made it to what was some type of camp or settlement that the German army had set up. It was some kind of transfer station positioned for the transfer of prisoners of war. I was unloaded from the jeep, as a German soldier kept a rifle pointed in my direction every second. I was taken to an area that was inhabited by what appeared to be many other prisoners of war. Most of them seemed to be from other countries. I didn't hear much English being spoken anywhere.

Even though I couldn't understand the talk of the other prisoners, I knew what they were feeling. It was similar to the look of the men back in our unit who had been chosen for scout duty, but much worse.

I thought my world had come to an end as I rode in the back of that large truck used for hauling prisoners. I felt like an animal being herded up and taken off to market. I felt like I was on the way to be slaughtered. I would learn later that I was not too far off the mark.

I anticipated that we were on the way to a prisoner of war camp, but to my surprise we stopped at the first town we came to. I had no idea why we were stopping. What would they want us to do in the midst of this German town? I soon found out.

They unloaded us again from the trucks, again making me feel like an animal. Guards would take any little opportunity to strike us. If they didn't feel like we were fast enough getting out of the truck, or didn't go fast enough to our marks, the guards would give us a little reminder as to who was in control here. They did this very often, much more often than was necessary. They seemed to get a big kick out of brutalizing us as we were lined up in the town.

We then proceeded to be paraded around the town. At first I just thought they might be giving us a chance to exercise. Maybe it was a long trip to the prisoner of war camp. Maybe the Nazis did have a heart after all. Was I ever wrong!

I soon realized the precise reason we were there in the town. We were being put on display as trophies taken by the Nazis. They wanted the people in the town to see that the German war machine was clicking on all cylinders. They wanted to put to rest any doubts the German people had as to who was winning the war. It was a huge propaganda move on the part of the Germans.

After I understood the Nazi motivation for bringing us here, I honestly didn't care. I wasn't in any hurry to get to any old German prisoner of war camp anyway. It didn't make any difference to me, that is until I saw the people of the German town and was the brunt of their reaction to us.

The people started screaming and yelling at us. Again, I couldn't understand most of what they were saying in their native German tongue. I didn't need to. I could tell how they felt about us. They were extremely angry with us, and at the urging of our German captors they became very violent.

They hurled obscenities verbally but did not stop there. They came at us with a vengeance. They got in our faces and yelled and screamed violently. They spat on us and many of them actually took swings at us. They were throwing bottles and other objects as we were paraded through the town. I, along with almost every one of the other prisoners of war, was hit several times by the people themselves or the objects they were hurling in our direction.

We were subject to this treatment and then loaded back into the truck, but I didn't realize that the displaying of us as spoils of war had just begun. We proceeded to stop at every town we went through for the next several miles. The only town that I remember by name was Cologne, Germany. We stopped at many towns including some in Belgium, near the German border.

It was extremely humiliating and degrading to be subject to this cruel mistreatment. It was also very dangerous. Many men were cut and bleeding from the blows that they received. We were fortunate to make it out of there with our lives.

I realized though that the Germans must have been very desperate to resort to these measures. They must have been frightened that the people of Germany had lost confidence in the Nazi war machine. The more that I thought about it the more I figured that actions like this must indicate that we were, in fact, winning the war. It made me feel a little better for the time being. It would be a long while before I would have very much to feel good about.

After they were finished parading us around for display, we finally made our way to a German prisoner of war camp. It was a very dark and drab establishment somewhere in Germany. I wasn't sure of the exact location, but I knew it was very near the German-Belgium border.

I could tell by the looks of the camp that the Germans definitely were not using much of their time on P.O.W. camp maintenance. It was awful. It made me sick just to look at it. I also knew what the next portion of my life was going to be like.

Very early in the educational process at basic training in Arkansas, we discussed the possibility of being taken prisoner. I remember listening to the instructions and not believing that it would ever apply to me. I thought some of the others in camp might possibly have to deal with this traumatic experience, but not me. No, it could never happen to me.

As we pulled into the camp, I remember trying to recall my instruction at basic. We were told that we were to only give them limited information. We were to give them our name, our rank, and our serial number.

We were to give them these three bits of information and nothing else. It sounded easy enough, but in reality we all knew it wasn't. It's very easy to talk about not giving out any more information when you're in Arkansas. It's a much different story when you actually find yourself in the midst of a prisoner of war camp in Germany facing interrogation by the Nazis.

I had heard all the horrible stories about how the Nazis would use all kinds of torture tactics to get information out of our troops once they were captured. If these stories were true, then it appeared that the Germans would stop at nothing to get Allied prisoners to talk.

I had always had some questions about the validity of these accounts. I just couldn't imagine anyone being so cruel. I wondered if the stories were fabricated, or at least exaggerated to encourage our troops to try to do anything possible to avoid capture by the enemy. I soon changed my opinion.

We were taken to our housing area where we were thrown into individual rooms, or cells. They were extremely tiny, with barely enough room to stretch out. It was very evident that the Nazis were trying to get the most out of their housing dollar. They tried to squeeze as many prisoners as they possibly could into a miniscule area.

We had been in our cells for only a few moments when guards started to take men away one by one. The prisoner would be dragged off to be "debriefed", so to speak. Most of the men went without much fanfare, but some raised quite a fuss. They probably were the ones who knew exactly where they were headed.

The guards squelched any disturbance very quickly and convincingly. After a few men resisted they were beaten severely. This went on for a while, but after a few beating displays it pretty much stopped. I guess the men felt that they were going wherever the guards wanted to take them anyway. It only caused them more pain and grief by resisting the inevitable.

After seeing some men return from their "debriefing" it really didn't seem to matter too much whether you resisted or not. The ones that left the cell area without a scratch returned beaten to a pulp. I couldn't understand what the prisoners were saying since none of the men in the immediate area were American, but I could see enough to get the gist of what was going on.

They finally came for me. I thought momentarily about putting up a fight, but decided against it. As I said earlier, I knew I was going where they wanted to take me anyway, there was no use to resist it. I also didn't want to give the guards the opportunity to be able to beat me before I went. I saw the looks on the guard's faces as they were pummeling my fellow prisoners. They seemed to really enjoy dishing out the punishment. I didn't want to give them the satisfaction.

They led me to a room in another area of the camp. They sat me in a chair in the middle of the room. A German Captain entered the room with another German guard. The Captain walked around the room momentarily looking at me and smiling. He then proceeded to explain things to me.

He told me that they were in total control now. I no longer had my unit or officers to help me. He tried to make it clear to me that he wanted to make this easy for me. He said he wanted to be able to go through this process in a way that would be the most beneficial for both parties. He then very casually asked me what unit I was with.

I thought for a moment before I told him that I was sorry, Sir, and then gave only my name rank and serial number just as we were instructed to do. The German made his way slowly over to me. He then doubled his fist and proceeded to punch me in the face several times.

He put me through a very brutal beating as I continued not to answer his questions. He then started to use some of the Nazi propaganda techniques on me. He talked about how foolish that I was being to put myself through all of this for my country. He talked about how my country didn't care about me and that I was doing all of this for nothing. The German went on to denigrate about every aspect of our capitalistic government and of the American way of life.

After trying to "reason" with me for an extended period of time without any success, he went back to a more physical approach. He continued to beat me severely. He would punch for a few moments and then question me. When I wouldn't answer to his satisfaction, he would resume the beating. Part of me wanted to answer his questions so that he would stop the hitting. I continued to respond with my usual "Sorry, Sir..."

I was bleeding, bruised, and it felt like I was severely injured. I really thought that he might kill me with that first interrogation. After being taken back to that cell in that condition, I sometimes wished he had killed me.

The beating sessions didn't stop there. They were held on a daily basis. Each day I was taken into the room and subjected to the same brutality. Day after day I went through this horror. I didn't think I could make it, but I did.

Chapter 12

The same routine continued for about a week, or so. After that time the German never summoned me into his interrogation room again. I guess he figured that it was no longer worth the effort. He must have been satisfied that I was not going to talk. He was right, I wasn't. I can honestly say that he could have very well killed me, but I was not going to give him the information he wanted.

The physical abuse at the hands of the Nazis eased, but the abuse in general did not. The verbal abuse was a constant. The guards would continue to berate us by word of mouth. They would talk about how pitiful our country was. They mentioned very frequently that we would not be prisoners here in the first place if the United States had not stuck their nose into Germany's business.

They always were taking any opportunity to build up the glorious German fatherland. They would go on and on about the brilliance of their leader, Adolph Hitler. They would talk about how he brought their country back after a huge economic depression. They talked about how he had built their armed forces back to a point of world dominance. Some of them may have still harbored a grudge after Germany's defeat in World War I. They seemed to show great pride in the fact that Germany was again a world power to be reckoned with.

The conditions and our general treatment while at the prisoner of war camp were a nightmare. The Germans just turned their nose up at the regulatory standards of treatment of prisoners of war by the Geneva Convention. They realized that there was absolutely no way for those regulations to be enforced.

Our day started extremely early in the morning. We were rustled out of our very primitive beds and herded out to the yard. We would then take part in a very extensive calisthenics program for our exercise, as if we wouldn't get enough without them, as I'll explain momentarily. We would be driven very hard during this exercise program. If you showed any signs of not participating wholeheartedly, you would find yourself being hit by the butt of a rifle. I guess the Germans probably wanted to keep us too tired to have any energy to plan an escape.

After our morning exercise routine, we would then get to take part in our meal. Notice I didn't say our morning meal, or one of our meals. This was the only meal we got all day. Our meal usually consisted of one slice of bread, that's right, one slice of bread! We usually were given a small cup of water, or if we were particularly fortunate that day, maybe a cup of hot tea. This meal was barely enough to keep a bird alive and was supposed to get us through an entire day.

Needless to say we didn't have any trouble with gaining weight during our stay. I saw several men come into camp built very burly if not stocky and before long they were thin as a rail. The ones of us who were thin to begin with didn't have much room to go down. Many of us began to almost look like skeletons as bones began to appear very clearly behind our skin.

This was simply another case of the Germans paying no heed to the Geneva Convention. The amount of food that we were being given was not just insufficient, or inadequate, it was cruel. I realized that neither I, nor any other human for that matter, could last long on this diet.

After our meal we were usually loaded onto a truck and shipped out to a farm in the area. We were then put to work in the farm fields. We did a variety of things. Most of the time we picked vegetables and fruits. It was very difficult and tiring work. There were a couple of other reasons that made the work even more frustrating to me.

One reason that the work was particularly hard to take was pretty obvious. You remember our meal, so you know that we were all pretty hungry as we worked. I guess it was kind of like putting a starving mouse in charge of the cheese. Those vegetables and fruits were pretty appetizing to a famished prisoner of war. It was awfully tempting to try to grab some of the produce that we were slated to pick and devour some of them ourselves.

There was only one thing preventing us from doing this – a crazed Nazi guard with a loaded rifle standing a few feet away. This served as a pretty good reminder not to steal the crops. I saw some men try to do it and end up with a bullet in them. The Germans were quick to shoot and ask questions later. I'm sure they used this as a good lesson for any prisoner who was thinking of doing the same. You had better be prepared to take a bullet if you got caught.

I have to add a little footnote to that. After saying how frightening that the German guards were and how we had witnessed men shot down for stealing fruit it's important for me to add that a lot of eating of crops did go on. You have to remember that hunger will cause men to do many crazy and daring things in life. We were all starving and most of us were willing to take the risk.

You had to be pretty sneaky about eating any of the produce. I'm sure that many of the men had their own routine of doing this. I would usually watch the guards very closely for a little while. When I noticed that it appeared that they were being pretty casual for a time period, I would grab the potato, or whatever kind of vegetable or fruit we happened to be working in that day. I would quickly stuff the produce into my shirt. I would then watch carefully and when I got the chance I would take a quick bite. I would do this quite frequently. I got pretty good at it I guess, at least I never got caught. I guess you already figured that out since I'm writing this.

It sure was awfully nerve racking though. The whole time I was eating the produce, I was scared that a German would spot me. It didn't make for a pleasant meal that's for sure. It just goes to show you what men will risk if they are hungry enough, and I was hungry enough.

The other reason that the work seemed particularly hard to take was the fact that we knew where the food that we were harvesting was going. It was going toward the German war effort. It was being sent out to help feed the German Army. It made me sick to think that I was actually being forced to help feed the Nazis. I knew that I didn't have any choice, but I still loathed it.

After working until sunset we would then be taken back to our quarters at the prisoner of war camp. I was usually extremely exhausted. They worked us in the hot sun for hours on end without any breaks to speak of. After a long day of that I was usually ready for bed.

This pretty much was our routine at the camp, day, after day, after day. It got very monotonous to say the least. With the lack of food and the overload of work, not to mention the incredibly unsanitary conditions, it seemed like I felt sick most of the time during my stay.

As much as I hated the abuse, food, and the working conditions, I think the worst thing about my time in the prisoner of war camp was the loneliness. I felt extremely lonely. I was the only American in the camp, at least to my knowledge. There may have been more, but I didn't get to see or meet them.

Most of the men didn't speak any English, with the exception of a few men who hailed from Great Britain. Our ranking officer was from England. I spoke to him a few times, but I never felt any kind of real closeness to him. I was unbelievably lonely at times.

The main reason that I felt a strong sense of helplessness while I was held captive was because I was not helping our country win the war. I sometimes felt guilty about this fact. I felt like I was no longer pulling my weight in the war effort. I had been careless in that French village and gotten myself taken prisoner and now I was no longer any use to our side. In fact, as I mentioned earlier, I was now actually providing a service to the Germans. I was helping to bring in produce that was going to help feed their troops. It was frustrating.

I was also very anxious because we didn't get to hear what was happening in the war effort. We didn't know if our troops had made it any farther into France. We didn't know what was happening on the German-Russian borders. We had no idea what was happening with our effort in the Southwest Pacific. It made for many anxious nights pondering what was going on.

I felt confident that things were going our way in the days right before my capture, but I knew that in war the tide could turn very quickly. It appeared that our men were firmly entrenched in France and heading toward the German border. It had sounded as if things were not going well for Germany on the eastern front either, but many days had passed since then.

The only news I got was from the German guards. They had radios that they would listen to. They would tell us that the Germans were winning the war. They would talk about the Nazis gaining victory after victory. We didn't really know whether to believe them or not. We acted like we did just to keep them happy and in a good mood so they wouldn't take any frustration out on us.

The most disturbing thing about some of the stories the German guards relayed was what they told me was happening in the United States. They told me that the Germans had bombed many major cities in the United States. They said that they had successfully completed bombing missions on New York, Washington D.C., etc. They told us that these major cities lay in ruins with thousands of Americans killed.

Again, I didn't know whether to believe them or not. I knew that it was a distinct possibility. We had heard many rumors about German subs that had been possibly spotted just off the East Coast. These Nazi submarines were supposedly loaded with missiles and were targeting the United States mainland. We had heard these stories earlier in the war, but they were never confirmed.

We had also heard stories about a German "super weapon" that was supposed to be in the works. I didn't know any details about this, but I wondered if they had come up with something that could hit our mainland. I really didn't know whether to believe the Germans or not, but it definitely gave me an eerie feeling to hear.

I thought about many things as I lay in my bed during my stay in the prisoner of war camp. I thought many nights about my home back in Southern Illinois. I wondered if they even had any idea that I had been taken captive. I figured that the Army might let them know if they could. Then I thought about it and realized that the Army probably didn't even know. They may have listed me as missing in action, but they had no way of knowing for certain that I was taken prisoner.

This made me wonder if they thought that I was dead. I wondered if they might send word back to my family of my demise. I hoped that they hadn't done that. I also hoped that if they had sent word back that I had been killed, that my family wasn't too upset. Actually I guess I hoped they were.

I thought a lot about Rose and the men of my unit. I wondered what Rose had thought about our situation in the village. He had left me in apparent good shape only to return and have me be nowhere to be found. I hoped he wasn't feeling that he might have done something wrong, because he hadn't. He had every reason to believe that I was in good shape and he had to get the word back to the unit. The survival of the unit was much more important than the survival of one man.

I found myself wondering where the unit had progressed to in France. I pondered whether they were in the midst of any fierce battles. I wondered whether any of the members of the unit had been killed. I thought mostly about Rose. I wondered how he was doing without his number one scout. I hoped he was doing fine. I sure wished that I was with him and the unit.

I sometimes got very depressed about my situation. There really didn't seem to be too much to look forward to. I longed to be back with Rose and the men of my unit. I found myself in a desperate state. I even contemplated a breakout attempt. I tried to think of a plausible way to get out, but could never come up with a plan that had a very realistic chance of success. As much as I wanted out of there, I figured that an attempt to escape was doomed to failure. It simply didn't seem like it was worth the risk. Then I overheard a conversation that changed my attitude.

I was out in the fields working one very hot afternoon when one of the German guards approached another. They paused and had a very noteworthy conversation that I accidentally overheard. One of the guards mentioned to the other German that he had heard tell of an idea on how to deal with the prisoners of war that the Nazis had taken in. He said that High Command in Berlin had come up with a plan to solve the prisoner problem. Evidently they felt like the numerous prisoners of war were costing them in the war effort.

The Nazi leaders evidently thought that the process of housing and feeding the prisoners of war was becoming too costly. This puzzled me because I couldn't figure how we were costing the Germans money. We were being housed in a facility that was not fit for anything else. The Germans certainly were not spending much if anything at all on upkeep. They absolutely were not using much money on our food rations that we were being given.

The more I thought about this, the more I believed that the German High Command must have been figuring things differently than I was. It seemed to me that we prisoners were actually very cost effective. We were fed very miniscule portions of food that could not be very costly. Maybe more importantly we served as free labor. We worked at picking crops to help get food to the German troops. This had to save the Nazis a lot of time and money.

There was one other factor that could prove to outweigh all the advantages that we prisoners provided the Germans. The biggest problem with running the prisoner of war camps was the fact that it took valuable men to run them. These troops were evidently desperately needed on the front lines. As the two Nazi guards talked about this fact it was now even more evident to me that the war must be tipping heavily in the favor of the Allies.

Then they got to the most disturbing part of the conversation. The guard then explained the plan that High Command had come up with. He said they were going to send large groups of prisoners to Berlin to be executed. That's right, executed. I could hardly believe my ears. Surely even the Nazis wouldn't go that far. As I pondered this, I knew that the Nazis had shown every sign that they would indeed go that far. If this report was true, then there was a very good chance that if I remained in this prisoner of war camp much longer then my chance of survival was minimal. I thought about the conversation that I had overheard and could come up with only one way to improve my chance of survival. I had to escape.

For the next few days I paid very close attention to what would seem to be small details of every part of camp life. I was looking for any opportunity that might present itself. I knew that just making a run for it, so to speak would be suicide. I had to come up with a plan that would at least have a chance for success. I surveyed the entire camp looking for any possible weakness in the security. I monitored the exact routine of all the guards, when they made rounds and bed check, etc.

After a few days, I finally noticed something. There was a milk cow that was being stored in a pasture adjacent to the camp. A German guard would milk the cow each day and then send it back into the pasture. There was also a large drum for storage that was located in the general vicinity of the field. I thought about all aspects surrounding the milking of the cow and surmised that this could be my opportunity for a potential getaway.

After I decided that this method of escape was indeed feasible, I decided to explain my plan to the ranking British officer. I went through the plan with him and he was not particularly impressed. He looked at me and called me a "crazy yank". He thought it was suicide for me to try it. I knew that he was probably correct and that I should listen to his advice not to try the risky plan for breaking out. I should definitely draw on the Captain's many years of experience and abort my plans in their infancy. That was definitely what I should do. I should listen to him. I didn't.

As much as I believed that the Captain was probably right, I just had to try. I couldn't stay there any longer without at least making an attempt. I kept thinking that I would rather be shot in the back while trying to escape than be sent to Berlin to be gassed by the Nazis. I devised the details of the plan and then put it into action.

I knew that my best chance of escape would come during an evening that was not particularly bright. It needed to be a cloudy, overcast day in which visibility was limited. It was frustrating for a few days, as each day seemed to be clear and bright.

This continued for several days until there finally came a day in which the evening was dark and cloudy. I knew that this was the day I had been waiting for.

It worked out very well because on that particular dark evening there were not many men in the yard. I waited for my opportunity and dashed behind the huge storage drum. I hid there for quite a while before the guard took the cow out for milking. I stayed behind the storage drum until the guard was finished with the cow. He then slapped the cow on the rear end and the cow headed for the open pasture.

At the precise moment that the cow passed by the drum, I jumped out from behind the drum and hooked up with the cow. I used the cow as cover between the guards and me. I then proceeded to walk with the cow toward the pasture.

The cow hid me from the view of the guards as long as I stayed precisely on step with the animal. I had planned to make the attempt on a dark day because of the general visibility and the fact that there would be no shadows extending behind the cow that would give me away.

The walk from the drum to the pasture seemed like it was miles and miles long. I was extremely tense and nervous. I knew that any unusual sounds would cause suspicion and bring the guards over in the direction of the pasture that would cause my discovery by the Germans. I also knew that if I were caught that I would be taken out and shot for trying to escape.

The cow kept making his way closer and closer to the pasture. I stayed in my position of cover. It seemed like it took forever, but we finally made it to the pasture. The cow went off into the open pastureland, while I made my way into the thick weeds of the field.

I stayed put for a brief moment. I looked back and saw that no one seemed to be looking in my direction. I then crawled for the next several yards until I got out of sight of the camp.

I then took off through the German countryside. As amazing as it seemed, my escape attempt had been successful.

Chapter 13

It took a few moments for what had just happened to actually sink in. My plan had actually worked. I had made it out of the camp. I had schemed and planned for so long to get to this day. It almost didn't seem real. I had spent so many nights thinking about this moment and what I would do, that I almost couldn't decide if I were actually only lying in my bed thinking about my potential escape.

This was real all right. It was hard to comprehend, but it was real. I was out of the camp. The plan that the British Captain thought would never work had actually gotten me out of the POW Camp. I was free!

Then it hit me that I was free, but only for a moment, if I didn't get moving. I didn't have time to celebrate, or my jubilation would get me a look down the rifle barrels of a Nazi firing squad. I still had what would prove to be the most difficult part of my escape ahead of me. I was free, but I was somewhere in the German countryside in enemy territory.

I knew that I would have approximately two hours before the next bed check. That would be the head start I would have on the guards. More importantly that would be the head start I would have over the dogs. I had to make good use of the precious time that I had before anyone would notice that I was if fact gone. I knew once they realized I was gone, they would come after me quickly and with a vengeance. The Nazis didn't look too kindly on American prisoners who tried to escape. I knew that if they caught me that I would be shot in the courtyard. They would use me as an example to the other prisoners not to be stupid enough to try the same thing.

The most difficult thing about planning an escape route was that I wasn't sure exactly where the camp was located. I did however, know that we were close to Cologne and I also knew the direction that Cologne was from where I was. I paid close attention to this as our group arrived at the camp.

I also knew that Cologne was located on the banks of the Rhine River. This was the same Rhine River that served as a natural border between Germany and Belgium. If I could just make it to Cologne, I could get to the Rhine River Bridge. If I could make it across that bridge, I would be in Belgium. This wasn't exactly as good as home, but it was a much more friendly territory than I found myself in now as I made my way across the German countryside.

I carefully made my way in the direction of Cologne. I had to be very careful because I knew that if I were spotted, I would be turned in to the Germans. There were I'm sure, more than a few Germans who would be glad to turn in an American escaped prisoner. I imagine that most Germans would take every opportunity to score some points with the Nazis.

It helped that it was now dark outside and I could keep myself pretty hidden and out of sight. It was a very tense time as I made my way into Cologne trying to avoid contact with anyone. I had no way of knowing exactly what time it was, but as I reached Cologne I knew that the eight o'clock bed check had probably come and gone. I was sure that the Germans had discovered that I was missing. There was no turning back now, even if I wanted to. They would shoot me now, even if I returned of my own free will, not that the thought ever even crossed my mind.

I knew that I would soon hear the barking of bloodhounds as they were put on my trail. I had watched those dogs in the camp and I knew that they could do their job and do it very well. I knew as hard as I tried to throw them off of my scent that eventually the dogs would pick up the scent and lead the Germans to me.

These things were rushing through my mind as I carefully made my way toward the water and saw the Rhine. I knew my only chance of survival was to get across that river and into Belgium and I had to do it fast.

I could see the Rhine River Bridge up ahead. It would have to be my means of getting across the Rhine. I made my way up to the bridge and saw a very ominous sight there at the entrance to the bridge – armed guards.

I guess I wasn't too surprised. After all, I didn't think the Germans just left their border to Belgium open to the public. I'm sure people would have been fleeing over it in droves.

I had to think. I had to come up with a way across that river. I had made it this far and I couldn't turn back now. I had to make it across the Rhine and into Belgium. It was my only chance at escape. After thinking about my situation for a moment, I realized that I had three options.

I could give up and hope that the Nazis would show mercy on me. I probably don't have to tell you how long I thought about that one. I knew that if I did that I was basically committing suicide.

I could try to get down to the banks of the river and swim across. I thought about this one for a good bit. It seemed pretty appealing momentarily. I thought I could make it down to the banks without being seen. I also thought I could probably make it into the water without causing any disturbance. At the time it sounded better than facing those guards.

The more I thought about it though, the more I believed that this too might be a suicidal attempt. I didn't know exactly how far it was across the Rhine, but I guessed it to be about a half a mile. I thought I could swim that distance in favorable circumstances, I thought, but I wasn't sure. What I was sure of was that the conditions were not going to be favorable. I wasn't familiar with the characteristics of the Rhine, but I knew that if it was anything like most large rivers back home that swimming in it can be extremely difficult. I had heard many stories of people drowning back home trying to swim in the river. It wasn't like a lake, or pond. There were strong currents and undertows that made it almost impossible to swim in. I assumed that the Rhine River was probably no different. I surmised that my chances of swimming across the Rhine River successfully were very very slim.

That left only one option. I had to try to get across the Rhine River Bridge and over into Belgium. To do this I would have to somehow avoid the German guards that were stationed at the entrance to the bridge. As I looked more carefully, I noticed that there were also guards stationed on the Belgium side of the bridge. My prospects of doing this successfully didn't seem very promising, but it was by far the lesser of the three evils that I was faced with.

I surveyed the situation for a moment. Then I finally heard them. I heard the faint barking of bloodhounds, bloodhounds that were hot on my trail. Time was running out. I had to make a decision and make it fast.

Then I noticed something. The Rhine River Bridge was a steel bridge with large girders underneath it serving as supports for the massive structure. I then got an idea. I decided that I would try to make it across the bridge by crawling along the bottom of the steel structure. I have to admit that I wasn't all that thrilled at my prospects of making it across, but it seemed to be my only chance and the faint barking of the dogs was getting less and less faint.

I then took off my belt and my shoes along with anything else that I thought would make the least bit of noise as I tried to get across the half-mile bridge. I then made my way down to the under parts of the bridge and climbed on. I then proceeded to start my trip.

For the first few moments everything seemed to be working just fine. I was swinging from girder support to girder support. I'm sure I made it through the first portion of the journey on pure adrenaline. The first few yards went very quickly, and then it hit me. The strength and energy that it took to swing across the bridge caught up with me. My arms felt like dead weight. I just couldn't go on any longer. I had to stop, or I was going to fall.

I paused for a moment and rested my sore arms. I rubbed them down feverishly trying to get the feeling and strength back in them. I knew that I needed to get going, but my body could only do so much.

I had to stop many times during the trip across the bottom of the bridge, but I finally made it to the Belgium side. I still had one more obstacle to face – the guards on the Belgium side.

I had to stop when I made it to the Belgium side of the bridge and rest for a few moments. The trip had absolutely worn me out. I needed to get a resurgence of strength and energy before I faced the last obstacle to making it safely into Belgium and out of Germany.

After I rested, I looked around the area to see what I was going to be faced with. Now, on the German side of the bridge there had been two guards walking along the entrance monitoring the huge structure. I expected the same on this side. I was only half right about that.

There were, in fact, two guards manning the Belgium side of the bridge, but they had company. There was also a tank regiment stationed there. I had been able to successfully elude the two guards on the German side of the bridge, but this was different. There were more men on this side, each man with two extra pairs of eyes that were honed in on the area.

I have to say that I was discouraged. I had been through so much to get to this point. I had made it out of camp by using what some would have called, and one did, a crazy scheme. I had made it through the German countryside and to Cologne. I had made it to the Rhine River Bridge just ahead of a group of bloodhounds that were zeroed in on finding me. I had found a way to make it across the

Rhine River Bridge by swinging from girder to girder like a monkey. Now I was faced with the prospects of trying to avoid contact with an entire tank company. It was difficult not to be discouraged by these events.

I decided that I should go quickly. I was afraid that the men would get word of my escape and be even more on the alert. I very slyly made my way out from under the bridge and to a brushy area, amazingly without being seen. The part of my escape that I had fretted about so much turned out to be rather easy. The men didn't seem to be paying particularly close attention. They evidently had not gotten word of the prison break. They didn't seem to be expecting anything, anything like an escaped American prisoner of war climbing out from the bottom of the bridge and heading into Belgium. Who could blame them? You'd have to be crazy to try something like that. Enough said.

Chapter 14

Thump, thump, thump. That was the sound my heart was making as it felt like it was going to bounce right out of my chest. I was so exited that I really didn't know what to do next. I had made it into Belgium. I was actually out of Nazi Germany and into the safer country on Germany's western border.

For the first time in quite a while I was not a prisoner. I didn't have to worry about following orders. I didn't have to worry about working all day in the fields. I didn't have to worry about sleeping in that poor excuse for a bed.

The best thing about making it out of the prisoner of war camp may have been the fact that I didn't have to eat the pitifully poor food there. Yeah, that was the best thing about it. The more I thought about it, I also realized that the worst thing about escaping was you guessed it, having to eat the pitifully poor food. It wasn't very long into the night before that small piece of bread and cup of water, or especially hot tea sounded awfully good.

It hit me for the first time that as bad as the prisoner of war camp was, they at least were providing food and water, as poor as it was. I would now have to come up with these items myself. I had an extremely difficult problem to have to deal with to survive. Did I ever wish I had not tried the daringly desperate escape?

Never! Not a chance! As hungry as I was and as thirsty as I would get, I never once reconsidered my decision to break out of the camp. I would have rather died from starvation or dehydration than die in that camp.

For the first few hours of my newfound freedom I ran at an extraordinary pace. I was running on pure adrenaline. I was so pumped up about my successful escape that I just ran. I wanted to get as far away from that German border as I possibly could. Even though I had made it across the border, I couldn't rule out the possibility of the Germans tracking me into Belgium.

Although I was very glad to make it out of Germany and into Belgium, I knew that the area of Belgium near the German border was well in the range of occupation by the Nazis. It was currently a battleground and the Germans had been forced back toward its own border, but the Allies had not made it that far into Belgium at that time. I was by no means out of the woods, yet.

As morning light began to dawn, the incredible amount of energy that I had expended in the escape, both physical and mental, started to catch up with me. I wanted to keep going, but my body said stop. I fought it for what I figured was a few miles and then I had to give in to it. I had to think rationally.

I knew I was many, many, miles away from the safety of any Allied troops. As much as I wanted to get to the American, or even British front lines, I knew that I couldn't make it there tonight. I didn't really know how far away I was. It might take me several days to get to friendly cover.

I used the sun coming up to help me go in the right direction. I wasn't sure of the exact location of our lines, but I knew common sense told me to head west, so I did. As I headed in the opposite direction of the rising sun, I began to see the countryside more clearly. I could see what land area I was up against. I also knew that just as the sun was brightening things up for me to see things, it was also casting more light on me. This would greatly increase my chances of being seen.

I knew that there were most certainly Nazi regiments in Belgium. I figured that they were more scattered than inside the German border, but I knew they were there. I knew that if a unit spotted me, that I was as good as dead.

I also wasn't sure about the reaction of civilians in Belgium. I figured that most of them were probably not big fans of the Nazis. After all, the Germans were in their country, and not by invitation. I didn't know what would happen if civilians spotted me. I thought that they might actually help me flee the Nazis. I also was afraid that even though the Belgium people were probably not big fans of the Nazis, that finding an escaped American prisoner of war would be a good way to get on the good side of the Nazis occupying the country.

I couldn't take the chance. I had to make sure that I was not seen. I was also exhausted. I took a few moments and thought about the situation I was in. As much as I wanted to go on, as much as I wanted to get to our lines, I knew I had to stop. I had to rest. I just could not go on any longer. Combining this with the fact that I couldn't risk being seen made me come up with my game plan.

I would stop and stay put during the day. I would find a good spot to hide out during the day. I would use this time to rest up and revive myself. I would then wait for the sun to go down and then make my move. I would then try to cover as much ground as I could while the sun was down.

I found an area out in what looked like the middle of nowhere. I gathered some mud and leaves and covered myself in them. I then proceeded to sleep. I first thought that I might be too excited to sleep, but I was wrong.

As I lay in that mud and leaves, I very quickly fell asleep. The next thing I knew, my eyes opened and I surmised by where the sun was that I had slept most of the day. I was now refreshed and ready to go. I continued my trip through the Belgium countryside. I continued following the same pattern for the next several days. I would move all night, covering as much ground as I could, and then would find a spot in a deserted area and cover myself in dirt, leaves, and mud and sleep most of the day.

This system that I used helped deal with my problem of being seen during the daylight hours. It also seemed to solve my sleeping problem, but I had a couple of other big problems to deal with during my jaunt through Belgium. Unfortunately for me and my survival, these were two pretty big problems – food and water.

I realized that I could make it for several days without food, but only a matter of hours without water. I was lucky enough to find some water in some places along the countryside. I used a couple of small creeks and streams, and also a few ditches to help satisfy my thirst. Some of these were not exactly the most desirable means of liquid, but when you're desperate, you're desperate.

For the first couple of days I just headed west, but then I got a little help in this respect. I started to hear artillery and shelling off into the distance. This told me where the front lines were. This was a good sign. It meant that I was getting closer to our lines. There was also one more ominous realization that this meant. I was also getting close to the Nazi lines.

As I continued to head in the direction of the artillery sounds, I started to feel the effects of not eating for an extended time. I was weak, very weak. I was getting tired much more quickly than I had earlier. I was also not covering as much ground as I had when I first began my journey.

I was already somewhat weak and malnourished by my stay in the prisoner of war camp. Now I had gone for a few days without food and it was starting to show. I knew that if I didn't find some food and find that food fast, I wasn't going to make it much further.

I then found myself just on the outskirts of a rural area in Belgium. This area looked populated. There were a few houses in the immediate area. I had to be careful, but I had to approach them to try to find some sign of some type of food. I had no choice but to take the risk.

I waited for nightfall and then I made my approach. Then I got a big break. I found pay dirt. It was a garden. It was almost too good to be true, but that's what it was. The garden had many types of vegetables to feast on, and that's exactly what I did. I ate, and ate, and then ate some more.

When I was full, which was the first time I could say that in a very long time, I paused to think. I had to make good use of my find. I picked some more of the vegetables and stuck them inside my clothes. I knew that as full as I was right now, that I would soon be hungry again, and these garden treats would then come in very handy as I made my way toward the front lines. I picked enough to be able hold me over for a few days and then headed out before daylight. It didn't take too long for me to feel the positive effects of my delicacies.

I was fortunate enough to run on to a few more gardens during the next few days of my trip. It sure was good eatin'. It was eatin' that I had not done in a while. I tried not to eat too much. I didn't want to get sick, but it was difficult to stop. It's hard to describe how good fresh food tasted to me after all those months without it. It was absolutely wonderful.

As much as I loved the garden food, I couldn't let the fact of my indulgence effect my overall perspective. I had to pay attention to where I was at all times and stay out of sight. There were more times than I care to mention in which I was close to being spotted. I found myself in many instances where I had to stay in an area longer than I really wanted just to make sure the coast was clear. I knew that as much as I wanted to cover ground quickly, it was better to be safe than sorry. I knew that all I had done to get this far would be in vain if I were spotted.

One evening I was making my way through the countryside. I came upon a rural farmhouse. I took some time and cased the place. After an extended time, I came to the conclusion that the house was deserted. I didn't know why it was abandoned. I thought that this might be a sign that I was getting closer to the front. The fighting could have forced the family who occupied the house to flee Belgium. I also thought that it could be another instance of Nazi cruelty. They could have forced the family to leave their home, or even executed them. I wasn't sure, but I sure knew that the brutal Nazis were capable of anything.

When I was absolutely convinced that the house was vacant, I decided to have a look around. I thought, or maybe I should say I hoped that there might be some kind of leftover food. I was hoping for something other than vegetables, not that I was looking a gift horse in the mouth.

I appreciated the garden food, but I had a taste for something else. I really had a taste for meat, any kind of meat. Maybe it was the lack of protein in my body, I don't know. All I knew was that I sure was hoping that this family had left behind some type of meat for me to pilfer.

I looked around all over the place and found nothing. I looked the place up and down. I found nothing. Whatever the circumstances were surrounding the departure of the family, they must have had plenty of time to garner up all the food. Either that or the Nazis had finished off any food that was edible in the house because there was nothing, absolutely nothing. At least that's what I thought.

I had all but given up the search when I heard it. I heard a sound. I quickly found some cover. There was someone there after all. There had to be. I had heard a noise. I paused for a moment and waited. It was several minutes, but then I heard it again. It was the same sound. I again waited for what seemed like forever, though it was actually probably only a few seconds before I heard it again.

Was it the family that lived in the home? I couldn't let them find me, not after all I had been through. I couldn't let the family turn me over to the Nazis. Maybe it was the Nazis. Maybe they were using the deserted farmhouse as housing for troops. If they found me I knew what would be in store for me. It was a tense few minutes as I waited for a sign as to the source of this noise.

There it was again, but this time it was much closer. Whoever it was they were closing in on me. I had nowhere to go. I was caught. After all I had been through, I had let my guard down and gotten caught.

I waited a few seconds before I finally saw the dreaded sight. I saw the source of the noise. I was caught. I was caught, all right. A chicken caught me. That's right, I said a chicken.

I didn't know whether to laugh or cry. I had been so nervous. I had almost resigned myself to being caught. The chicken was a sight for sore eyes for two reasons. The first reason was obviously that there was nobody here. There were no family members left in the home. There were no Nazis there at the house ready to take me in to be executed by a firing squad.

The other reason was the simple fact that I was starved and I loved chicken. I mean I loved cooked chicken back home. It was a delicacy back home. I could just smell the fried chicken. This presented another problem. I had no way to cook the chicken. I couldn't risk starting a fire. There could be Nazi troops in the immediate area. If they saw my fire, it would lead them straight to me. No, as much as I would have liked to, I couldn't risk it.

That left me two options. I could just let the chicken go and only dream about the mouth-watering bird, or I could eat the chicken without cooking it at all. That's right, I could eat it raw. I know what you're probably thinking – Goodbye, Mr. Chicken. I guess it's your lucky day. It's a very good thing for you that I don't have any way of cooking you.

Before I tell you what I did, let me explain something to you. I was hungry, very hungry and I had a taste for chicken. At the time I would have preferred to have a nice fried bird, but I would have preferred many things that I didn't have. I decided to make the best of the situation.

I ringed the chicken's neck. For those of you who aren't familiar with this term, or only think it's a threat that your parents used against you when you were young, that means I broke it's neck. That's a nice way of saying that I killed it. I then carefully plucked the bird. After finishing preparing my meal, I then ate the chicken completely raw.

It would probably make a more exciting and adventurous story to say that it was the best chicken I ever ate. It wasn't. It was probably, however, the most satisfying chicken I ever ate. I wouldn't want to have to eat another chicken raw today, but I can honestly say that if I were faced with the same situation today that I would do exactly the same thing again.

I'm not sure that my stomach knew what to think about what had just been sent down to it. One reason for this was that the chicken was raw, and the other reason was that my stomach had not had any meat in it for so long that I'm sure my stomach thought that it was some kind of unknown substance.

After all these years and all the exciting stories that I tell of my World War II exploits, my accounts of eating the raw chicken may get the biggest response from kids that listen in.

After I finished eating, it was near morning. I found a good spot and rested. It was the first time I had gone to sleep on a full stomach for quite some time. As I said, it wasn't the best chicken I ever ate, but it sure hit the spot.

Chapter 15

As I've already stated, I was faced with many potential problems during my flee from Nazi captivity. I had been faced with the problem of food, which I had been fortunate enough to deal with pretty successfully. Between the gardens and my encounter with the chicken, I had eaten much better during most of my jaunt through Belgium than I had during my stay in the prisoner of war camp. I also had to deal with exhaustion. I did this by sleeping most of the daylight hours to rest up, and also the food that I came across helped strengthen me and gave me more energy to expend on my journey. I still had to be very careful, making sure I was not seen by anyone who might turn me over to the Germans. My system of moving only at night seemed to deal with this pretty successfully also.

As well as I had dealt with my problems up to that point, there was one more problem that was becoming an ever-increasing worry for me – the cold. It was now late fall and turning into winter very quickly. The temperatures were not brutally cold yet, but it seemed to get a little cooler each day. Winters in this part of the world are traditionally very bitter. I knew that the temperatures were only going to drop more with each passing day.

One would think that the temperature would be more difficult to take at night, with the sun going down, usually the temperature plummets also. This was probably true, but I actually had more trouble during the daytime. Even though the temperature was almost assuredly lower during nightfall, it didn't feel that way to me. You see at night I was active. I was constantly on the move. It made dealing with the temperature much easier.

At night, I also had my mind on other things. I was thinking about getting out of there. I was concentrating on making my way toward friendly troops and not thinking about how cold it was. This was another factor in helping me deal with the temperatures at night.

Because of this I actually had my biggest problem dealing with the temperatures during the daylight. Even though the temperatures were higher during the daylight hours, I wasn't active like I was at night and I felt the cold more.

The clothing that I was wearing definitely didn't help matters in my dealing with the weather conditions. My uniform had taken a beating during my stay in the prisoner of war camp. It was just barely holding together. It had holes in it from top to bottom and was actually little more than rags.

Even though I had great reason to worry about my impending problems, I can honestly say that for some reason, I didn't really fret about it too much. I didn't have time to. I had to keep moving. I had dealt with all my other problems, so I knew I would just have to deal with my problem with the weather conditions also. After having success in getting out of the camp and solving the problems I had faced before, I started to feel that something would help me deal with this problem, too. I almost felt like someone was watching over me. Indeed, they were.

I continued to make my way toward the artillery sounds that I would occasionally hear. The sounds were still very faint, but were growing less and less faint through the passing time. I knew I had to head in the direction of the sounds, but I also did so with a little apprehension, knowing that just as the sound meant our troops were in the general area, it also meant that there were Nazis there, too. I would find this fact to be true all too soon.

One particular night as I was on the move, things didn't seem to look too promising to me. The temperatures were continuing to plummet. Where at one time I was able to keep moving and stay warm during the nighttime hours, now even the exercise didn't seem to help. I was getting colder and colder by the minute. I knew that I couldn't last too much longer.

That night, after battling the cold, I paused for a moment. I saw something up in the distance. I wasn't quite sure what it was. I carefully made my way closer to the objects that I viewed from afar. It became more and more apparent to me what I was seeing. It was the Nazis.

I stopped cold, pardon the pun. I hid myself as best as I could without making any noise. I then watched. It appeared to be a German unit of infantrymen. I couldn't see things particularly clearly, but it looked as if the men in the unit that I saw were all asleep.

I found this to be rather strange. I thought maybe I could only see one group of the unit and that the others were up and on guard duty. I knew that no unit would let all the members sleep at the same time and leave themselves open for any kind of hostile attack from the enemy.

I continued to peer at the seemingly slumbering Nazis. I watched for what seemed like hours. There continued to be no movement from the men. I couldn't believe it. I just couldn't believe that the men of the unit would still be sleeping. It was now well into the morning and they continued to sleep.

I slowly and methodically made my way closer to the unit to get a better look at just what was going on. I could now see that the men were not only apparently sleeping, but they weren't moving at all. In fact, to my knowledge the men of that German unit had not as much as moved one muscle since I discovered them and began watching them several hours ago.

I continued to watch and watch. There was no movement whatsoever from the men of the unit. After a while, I finally came to the conclusion that the men were not asleep after all. They were dead.

I carefully walked into the camp of men. It was a small unit of Nazis, and as I thought, they were all dead. I wasn't sure what had killed them. There was no obvious sign of means of death. All I knew for sure was that they were dead.

I started to leave the unit and continue heading in the direction of the now more audible artillery sound when I got a thought. I had been dealing with the cold weather conditions for several days now. It was starting to catch up to me. I was in danger of some type of hypothermia if I continued in this state. I had a means of help right in front of me. There were many dead Nazi soldiers lying there in that camp. They were clothed in what were the thickest, warmest, uniforms that I had seen in a while, at least their German uniforms appeared that way in comparison to the rags that I was currently wearing at the time.

It seemed like an easy leap to make. I should just take one of the likely gassed German uniforms and put it on. It would be immeasurably warmer than my American threads that I was clad in.

There were some problems to this plan. I know it may sound a little petty now, but I just didn't want to put that uniform on. I just couldn't bring myself to donning the Nazi uniform. It stood for so much that I was against. It was a symbol of everything that I was fighting to abolish. As much as I wanted to, there seemed to be no way that I could make myself put that uniform on.

Just then a dose of reality hit me pretty hard as a strong north wind hit the holes in my uniform. It chilled me to the bone. I thought for a moment and then grabbed the German uniform and put it on over my uniform. I got kind of a sick feeling just putting it on, but it was a warm sick feeling.

I was having kind of a difficult time dealing with wearing the uniform until I started to think about it in more detail. I finally came to the conclusion that it was a sense of positive irony as I realized that the Nazis were actually helping me survive. It helped me deal with the uniform.

I now had an even stronger sense that I was being looked out for. I had been faced with so many problems, only to be given a way to deal with each successive problem. This had happened several times already in my escape and journey. I almost was coming to expect it.

I continued toward the artillery sounds. I then for the first time saw some definite signs of battle. I had been hearing artillery sounds for many miles, and had had my run in with the dead German soldiers, but this was the first live sign of battle. I saw planes flying overhead. They weren't just planes. They were our planes.

I assumed that the planes were on their way to a bombing mission. They were most likely on their way inside the German borders. They may have been headed to Cologne, or maybe Hamburg. Wherever they were headed, it was a very welcome sight for me to see at that time.

I knew that I must be headed in the right direction. I continued to hear the now not as faint artillery sounds. I had stumbled on the German unit, and now I had witnessed some of our planes on their way to bomb Germany. It was encouraging to see that I was getting closer.

As I continued my trek across the Belgium countryside, I saw a small farmhouse off into the distance. I decided to inspect it. I wanted to see if there was a garden, or any sign of food. I also wanted to see if the house was deserted, or not. That might give me an indication as to how far from the front lines that I was at that particular time. I made my way closer to the home.

I looked around the area of the farmhouse for a moment. I didn't see anyone, but it looked as if someone might live there. I nosed around a little to see if whoever lived there was still there, or if they had been forced out by the battle. I then continued looking around, now pretty confident that nobody was around. I would soon find out how wrong I was.

A few moments later I made my way around a corner of the farmhouse. I had kind of let my guard down somewhat thinking that the farmhouse was unoccupied. Then I saw them. The small farmhouse was sure enough occupied, and there they were. It was two women.

I froze. So did they. It seemed for a moment that time had actually stood still. Upon seeing me their eyes proceeded to get as big as silver dollars. I couldn't see my own eyes, but I'm sure they were just as big. I was just as frightened, as it appeared that the two women were.

One of us then yelled, and I'm afraid that it very well might have been me. We both took a long step back, intensely staring at the surprising sight of the other. I was afraid that the women would turn me in, as I'm sure that the two women were just as afraid that I was there to do them harm.

After a very awkward pause, the two women started conversing with each other. I couldn't understand a word they were saying. They would speak, sometimes in an almost hysterical manner to each other. They would then look at me for a while. I noticed that they kept pointing toward my uniform.

I then realized that they were trying to decide not only who I was, but also more importantly what side I was on. I'm sure they had no idea since I was wearing a German uniform over an American one. I would imagine that they were extremely confused by this.

I'm sure you've heard what most Americans think about the English language in regards to using it with people who understand none of it. Most of us think that everyone in the world understands English if you speak it slowly enough. I sometimes laugh now when I think about it, but that's what I tried initially. I tried to let the two women know that I was an American and more importantly at that moment that I was not there to harm them in any way.

I was getting nowhere in my verbal explanation, but the ladies seemed to be calming down slightly. They continued to talk to each other and then look at me. I'm sure it didn't take them too long to realize that I was down on my luck to say the least. I was pretty filthy, unshaven, and probably looked pretty bad all around after my long stay in the prisoner of war camp and now going through the last several days on the run through Belgium.

The two women seemingly started to look more at ease with me. Maybe they could tell from my manner and body language that I wasn't a threat to them. I also picked up from their manner that it didn't appear that they had any great desire to rush somewhere to turn me in.

The women looked at me with very caring smiles. I couldn't understand what they were saying, but I knew that it must be good. The two women then very gently took me aside and offered to help me.

They gave me something to eat and also to drink. The food tasted great and it was the first time in a very long time that I had had anything but water to drink. They gave me a very nice tasting wine. I think I would have enjoyed drinking just about anything at that moment, but I have to admit it was particularly enjoyable to partake in something other than water.

The women continued to dote on me for the next several minutes. I definitely didn't hurry out of there. It was the first human contact I had had, with living bodies that is, since I left the prisoner of war camp. Come to think of it, it was really the first human contact I had had since I was captured. You couldn't really call anything about my dealings in that prisoner of war camp as human.

I found my short stay with the two women to be absolutely delightful. They showed a lot of caring and compassion. They had after our initial meeting, showed no concern as to who I was, or what side I was on. I'm sure they never really knew for sure where I stood. Honestly, they just didn't seem to care. All they seemed to care about was that it looked as if I need help, and they helped me greatly. They saw a human being in need and they did something about it. It was sure a refreshing sight to behold there in the midst of all the battles and bloodshed that was all too prominent at that time in that area of the world.

It was very difficult for me to leave. The ladies didn't seem to want me to hurry off, but I knew I had to go. I needed to move on and I would probably only put those nice ladies lives in more danger by staying. I was sure that if the Nazis found out that they had helped an American escaped prisoner that they would likely be shot. I didn't want to put their lives in any danger.

As I tried to make it clear to them that I had to go, they wanted me to take some rations of food with me. If it were up to them, they would have given me their whole food supply. I had eaten plenty and didn't want to leave the two nice ladies short of food that they might need later. The drink that they gave me was so good though that I did take them up on their offer to take a bottle of it with me.

I said an emotional goodbye to the two ladies and took off again in the direction of the battle sounds. I don't know what happened to those nice ladies after I left. Hopefully they escaped any more hardships brought on by the war, and were able to lead peaceful lives. I will always be indebted to those two women.

They showed me much about the human spirit. They were willing to help a tired and hungry soldier and they paid no attention to sides or nationalities. It would be a great lesson for us all to heed.

As I made my way away from the farmhouse, I continued to hear the artillery sounds, only now they were much more audible than ever before. I then saw a group of United States planes fly overhead, again, I'm sure on their way toward targets inside Germany. I then heard a barrage of gunfire from the ground. Evidently there was a German artillery unit stationed not too far away.

The planes continued to fly over as the Nazis also continued to fire at them. I then saw one of the planes burst into flames. The Germans had a hit. The plane proceeded to sputter and head toward the ground. I got a very sick feeling as I found cover and watched that plane head toward the earth at an alarming rate. I was helpless to do anything but watch.

I noticed a small object in the sky. I then saw a parachute open. The pilot had made it out of the plane, apparently safely. He continued to float toward the ground. I decided to head in that direction. I thought I might be able to help the downed pilot. I also welcomed the company.

I then started to hear more gunfire from the ground. I couldn't believe it, but it appeared that the Germans were shooting at the falling pilot. There were then some more shots toward the parachuting aviator. It was absolutely inhumane. It was just another in a long line of German violations of the Geneva Convention.

I waited for a moment hoping against hope that the pilot would elude the bullets, but he was absolutely helpless. I then saw his head drop. He had been hit. The Nazis had actually shot a defenseless pilot. They had no honor at all. It made me angrier than I think any of the other atrocities on the part of the Nazis that I had witnessed up to that point.

Most of the planes made it over the area successfully. The Germans managed to shoot down a few. Of those few that were shot down, they fired at all the pilots as they made their way to the ground after evacuating their doomed plane. I'm not sure how many of them were hit, but I know some were.

It was difficult to keep my composure after what I had just witnessed. I was still angry. I found myself almost wanting to hunt the Nazis down and make then pay for their brutality instead of avoiding them. I knew that if I let my anger dictate my actions that it would be suicide. The best way for me to get back at the Nazis would be for me to make my way back to my unit and reclaim my scout job. This would do more to help our war effort than anything else I could do at the moment.

I was at that time buoyed by the fact that I was evidently close to the front lines. I had to keep my guard up now more than ever. At any time I could come into contact with the Nazis and this time they would most assuredly be alive.

I continued to move and cover as much ground as I could that night after a very emotional day. I could now hear the artillery very clearly. I was what now appeared to be a short distance from the front. I had to withstand the urge to keep going even after sunrise. I was anxious to get to our troops, but I knew that before I got to our troops, I would have to get through the Nazis.

Knowing that I had to be even more cautious than ever, I made myself rest. I found a very secluded area, at least that's what I thought at the time. I covered myself in mud and leaves and laid down for a much-needed rest.

I seemed to be resting pretty comfortably until I started to feel something poking at me. I then awakened. I opened my eyes to find myself looking up at the barrel of a bayonet pointing right at me.

Chapter 16

For a moment I had hoped that the bayonets and the men that were holding them pointed directly at me were part of a horrible nightmare. I was still hopeful that I would wake up any moment sleeping peacefully in the pile of cedar leaves that I had used for cover. Unfortunately this was no dream and the bayonets and the men holding them were very real.

It was absolutely the ultimate in frustration. I had devised my plan of escape from the prisoner of war camp. I made my way to Cologne and to the Rhine River. I then, while dodging German guards, somehow managed to scale the width of the large steel structure by swinging along the bottom of the bridge to the Belgium side. I then eluded a tank squad and escaped into Belgium. I had roamed the Belgium county side for many days, avoiding being captured, only to face the end of a bayonet.

When I decided to try to break out of the prisoner of war camp, I knew very well the consequences I would face if caught. I was well aware of what the Nazis did to escapees. They were shot. I knew that was the fate that I was faced with. I was going to be taken back to Germany and executed.

One might think that I would now have second thoughts about my escape attempt and that I might reconsider whether I had done the right thing. It would seem pretty normal, with what I now found myself faced with. I was now certainly facing death. I can honestly say that I never had one second thought about my escape attempt, not one. Even though I was seemingly facing a firing squad and execution by the Nazis, if I could have gone back, I would have done exactly the same thing.

At first I paid very little attention to the men who were now leading me through a wooded area. The one thing that I noticed was the way that they looked at me. It was an extremely fierce look. It seemed that they were glaring a hole right through me. I could feel the utter disdain that they felt for me. It was very noticeable and much worse than any I had felt during my stay at the prisoner of war camp. Don't get me wrong, I was treated very brutally and inhumane during my stay at the prisoner of war camp, but what I'm talking about is the feeling of sheer hate I felt from these men. I could tell that these men that now held my fate in their hands probably would just as soon shoot me on the spot than look at me.

I then started to look over the men more carefully. They didn't look like the Nazis I had seen. They were definitely not in the usual Nazi uniform. Maybe they were working undercover trying to infiltrate the enemy.

Then I started to listen to them. They definitely didn't sound German, either. At least they weren't speaking in anything close to any German dialect I had heard. I didn't speak much German, but I had heard it spoken more than my share during my stay in the prisoner of war camp.

I started to listen more carefully to the men as they conversed with each other. I was no language expert, but I was pretty sure they were speaking French. The more I listened, the more I was convinced of it. These men were either Germans who were working undercover as Frenchmen, or they were actually French.

I wanted to hope against hope that these men were actually French, but I just couldn't believe it. They must be Nazis. They had to be. Why else would they take me in? The French were very sympathetic to the American liberation operation in their country. If they were French then they would have no reason to have any quarrel with me or any other American.

After waiting momentarily to be sure that the men were apparently French, I asked them of their nationality. I simply asked them if they were French. I waited for an answer before getting a sarcastic response. They were French all right. What a break! I thought I was on my way to Germany to be executed and come to find out the men who had taken me in were Frenchmen.

Still I had the question that continued to burn inside me – If these men are from France, why did they violently apprehend me? What reason would they have to bring me in? After all, we're on the same side.

I then finally got up the nerve to ask the men why they brought me in. I asked them what I had done. I told them that we were all on the same side. The men then gave me a very cynical stare and burst into laughter. They seemed amused for a moment before that amusement turned sour. That same stare that they had for me earlier was back. Then they puzzled me by their response to my comments, which ended with them referring to me as a Nazi.

Nazi? Did I actually hear them right? Did they refer to me as a Nazi? I must not have heard them correctly. My French had let me down. But, I then thought that Nazi was Nazi in French or American. They had referred to me as a Nazi, me, Cecil Rains from Pittsburg, Illinois, U.S.A. The same Cecil Rains that had just spent time in a Nazi prisoner of war camp. If anyone on earth shouldn't be mistakenly referred to as a Nazi, it was me.

I would have thought that this was some kind of a joke under normal circumstances. They must be just pulling my leg. They might be trying to put one over on the frightened American. I could tell very easily that this was no joke. They were very serious and so were their guns.

I spent the next few moments trying to figure this odd turn of events out. Then it hit me. It hit me like a ton of bricks as I looked down at my uniform, my German uniform. That explained things. How could I be so stupid? I had totally forgotten about the uniform. I was dressed in a German uniform. No wonder they thought I was a German soldier.

I then tried to go into an explanation as to why I was in a German uniform out in the Belgium countryside. One good thing about my attempt was that at least some of them seemed to speak English. I proceeded to go into the whole story.

I told them that I was an American who had just escaped from a Nazi prisoner of war camp. I talked about how I hid behind a cow and just waltzed right out of the camp. I relayed how I had made it to Cologne and scaled the bottom of the Rhine River Bridge and into Belgium.

I then explained to them how I managed to end up in a German uniform. I told them how I came across the dead Germans and had stolen their attire. I would like to tell you that they immediately believed me, that I had convinced them of how I had gotten into this particular situation. I would like to tell you that they bought it. Would you have believed it? – Me, neither.

The next several minutes were some of the more frustrating moments of my life. After all I had been through, it was so ironic that I was now faced with the compelling notion of either being able to convince these Frenchmen of my story being legitimate, or actually being executed by an ally.

I tried every way I knew to convince them. I told my story and then retold it. I tried relating it to them from every possible angle that I could. I just had to make them believe me. I just had to.

They paused at intervals and discussed me among themselves. I didn't know what they were saying, but I knew from the looks on their faces that I was getting that it didn't seem as if I was making any headway.

Then the pleading on my part turned into a sort of interrogation. It was actually very similar to many of the scenes of interrogation that I have seen on movies and television over the years since. They started to ask me questions. They started to ask me things that they thought that any American should know.

It was usually played out in this same manner on the screen. The interrogators would ask the accused spy these classic questions about the United States of America. These were the same types of things that the Frenchmen started to ask me. They asked me who the heavyweight champion of the world was. They asked me who had won the World Series.

I have always wondered why this sort of thing was done. I always questioned the validity of this form of evaluation. It just seems to me that any spy worth his weight would school himself in these aspects of American life. It just didn't seem to be a valid way to decide where a spy's loyalty lied.

It took me many minutes of fast-talking, along with staring down the barrel of a rifle, but I finally seemed to convince them. I don't think they were absolutely sure because they kept the rifle on me the entire time of my stay. I didn't blame them at all for that. I probably would have done the same thing if I were in the same situation that they were in. All I cared about was that we were heading to American lines where I would be turned over to the Americans.

Even though the Frenchmen kept the rifle handy, they did loosen up just a bit. I found out what organization they were with. They were from the F.F.I., which stood for Forces Francaises de l'Interieur, or Free French Interior. I later found out more about the intriguing history of the group.

In June of 1940, with a Nazi takeover looming, the control of the government of France was constitutionally given over to Marshal Philippe Petain, who concluded that France should sign an armisticc with Nazi Germany. This would in essence pave the way for Nazi occupation of France. Though many French loyalists disagreed, the armistice was signed.

General Charles de Gaulle, who had to flee France after Petain took power, then appealed to his countrymen by radio from London. The General called for a continuation of the French war effort against Germany.

On June 28, 1940 de Gaulle was officially recognized by Great Britain as the leader of Free France, as the resistance movement became referred to. The General then began the process of building his forces from his base in London. Early on these forces consisted of troops in England, volunteers from the French community, and a few units of the French Navy.

De Gaulle's forces began to expand. In the fall of 1940 the French territories of Cameroun, Chad, French Equatorial Africa, Moyen-Congo, and Oubangi-Chari, which were all African territories, united with Free France. Soon after, French colonies in India and the Pacific joined in also.

The Free French movement then began to establish itself as a legitimate part of the war effort. In 1941 Free French forces helped in the British operations against Italian forces in Egypt and Libya. Later that same year they again joined the British in defeating Vichy forces in Lebanon and Syria.

In September of 1941 de Gaulle set up the Comite National Francais, or the French National Committee. This was basically a Free French government set up in exile. The Allied governments then recognized it.

The Free French movement remained a relatively small force until 1942 when an underground anti-Nazi movement sprung up inside the occupied French border. De Gaulle recognized that he desperately needed the support of these forces inside France. In his efforts to gain their support, de Gaulle changed the name of the movement to Forces Francaises Combattantes, or Fighting French Forces.

De Gaulle then sent in his emissary Jean Moulin inside France to try to set up and unify all the French resistance forces under the leadership of de Gaulle. Moulin then set up the Conseil Nationale de la Resistance or National Council of the Resistance to help unify the resistance.

De Gaulle then became involved in a power struggle with the commander in chief of the French forces in North Africa, General

Henri Giraud. In June of 1943 the Comite Francais de Liberation Nationale, or French Committee of National Liberation was constituted. De Gaulle and Giraud were made joint presidents of the newly established group.

Giraud proved to be no match for the very savvy, de Gaulle. De Gaulle soon outmaneuvered Giraud, who resigned in the spring of 1944. Giraud's exit left de Gaulle in control of the entire Free French war effort outside of the French borders, while more and more Resistance groups inside of France began to fall in under de Gaulle's leadership.

I had heard of de Gaulle's efforts on behalf of France, but I had no idea how extensive those efforts were. More than 100,000 Free French troops fought in the Anglo-American operation in Italy in 1943. At the time of our invasion in Normandy in June of 1944, the Free French Forces had grown to well over 300,000 regular troops.

Our own government in the United States had been the greatest supporter of the resistance. De Gaulle's forces were almost totally equipped and supplied by the Americans. It proved to be a very effective decision on our part. The French Forces proved to be incredibly effective in our own war effort in France.

In August of that year the Free French First Army played a very significant role in the liberation of France by the Allies. The Free French First Army, under the direction of General Jean de Lattre de Tassigny, took part in the Allied invasion of Southern France. The Army then took part in the northeast drive into Alsace. The Free French First Army would then eventually join the Western Allies in the final thrust into Germany later in the conflict.

Also in August of that year, the Resistance groups, who were now referred to as Forces Francaises de l'Interieur, or French Forces of the Interior had mounted an organized anti-Nazi insurrection in Paris. General Jacques-Philippe Leclerc moved into Paris to consummate the attempted liberation of the French capital. I later found out that in late August of 1944, that General Charles de Gaulle, after several years of efforts, entered Paris in triumph.

At this point there was still much work to do to completely liberate France. The fall of Paris wasn't the end of German occupation in France. It was, however, the beginning of the end of the Nazi regime there.

After hearing of his exploits, I found myself intrigued by the exploits of General de Gaulle in his efforts to liberate his homeland. These men who had captured me were part of his resistance movement. I was especially enthralled by the incredible dedication of these men in their pursuits. You could just see the dedication in their eyes. They were truly passionate about their duty. It was nice to see the heart felt desire of these men to do all they could, including risk their lives to liberate their beloved homeland. History has proved that it is indeed very difficult to defeat a force that is passionate about what they are fighting for. Our country later would find this fact to be all too true in our doomed efforts in Vietnam.

I found myself feeling a sense of extreme closeness to these freedom fighters. I felt this way even though I was still looking down the barrel of a rifle. Actually this aspect helped me feel even closer to them. It showed how dedicated they were to doing whatever was necessary to perform their duty. I respected them very much for that fact, and I was also very glad that they were on our side.

They took me about two miles away to the American front lines. The F.F.I. then turned me over to the 28th Infantry Unit. This unit would then be responsible for transporting me back to Hurtigen Forest for processing.

Chapter 17

Free at last! Free at last!

I could hardly believe that after all I had been through that I was finally a free man. I had made it against all odds back to the American forces stationed in Hurtigen Forest, Belgium. It seemed almost too good to be true.

Hurtigen Forest meant Black Forest. It was so named because of the extreme darkness of the wooded area. It was said that the sun never touched the ground of that dense forest.

I was given a warm welcome from the men in the area who had learned of my return. It made me feel very good. I felt so very fortunate to be back. It had not actually sunk in yet.

The first thing that they did for me after my welcome was to let me sit down to a meal. Even though I was actually very fortunate to get the food supply that I managed to get while on the run, this was my first real sit down meal in I didn't know how long. It was great. I don't think that a meal had ever tasted so good to me. I ate and ate and then ate some more. I definitely overindulged.

After I finished my meal, I was taken to meet with some officers. I was then debriefed in the meeting. They wanted to know everything they could about my experience. They asked me about my capture in the French village. They wanted to know why the Germans surprised me the way they did and how I was taken in.

I told them of my experiences on the way to the camp. I relayed to them the story of how I was paraded through the towns we passed through in Belgium and Germany. They were interested in the people's brutal reaction to us as we were shown off as Nazi trophies.

I told the officer of the location of the prisoner of war camp near Cologne. I told them how I thought I was the only American at least that I knew of in the camp. I mentioned to them of the makeup of the nationalities of the prison population. They were very interested in the fact that I thought I was the only American there.

I then relayed to the officer the brutal beatings that I endured for the first week or so of my stay. They had had other accounts of this mistreatment, but evidently not too many got out to tell of the happenings inside the prison camps in Nazi Germany. The men debriefing me were understandably angered at the brutal treatment that I had to go through at the camp.

I told the men of our daily routine. I relayed to them how we mainly worked on a farm that was very close to the prison of war camp. This gave them even more of an indication of the exact location of the prisoner of war camp.

They were particularly interested in the information that I had overheard about the possible mass murder of prisoners of war. They were pretty sure that it was probably just a rumor, but like me, they were not sure of anything when the Nazis were involved. They thought as inhumane and brutal as the mass murder sounded, in this case, it could very well be true.

The men were also particularly amused at my means of escape. I told them about the cow and how I used it as a cover. They thought that was pretty funny.

I then relayed all my exploits on my way out of Germany and how I managed to scale the Rhine River Bridge. I also mentioned my run in with the dead Germans and with the live ladies. They seemed particularly impressed with my survival skills. I told of how I ate out of the gardens and even the raw chicken. I then told them how I met up with the Free French Forces.

I wasn't too thrilled with reliving my experiences so quickly after surviving my journey, but I knew why it was important for me to do so. I knew that intelligence used this information to help our units and men learn more about the enemy and their ways so they could better prepare for combat against them.

Soon after I was finished with my very lengthy debriefing sessions at Hurtgen Forest, the officials there congratulated me. I was then given some very astounding news. I was being sent home.

I was told that this was a common practice. They told me that if a soldier was captured and then was able to make it out and return, then they were sent back to the states. I questioned them as to why this was. They said that it was unfair to the man who had been captured to ask them to go back into combat for a few reasons.

One reason was that they believed that any soldier who had been captured and was put through the brutality of a stay in a prisoner of war camp deserved to be relieved of their responsibilities. The leaders thought that these men had more than done their duty and didn't deserve to have any more asked of them.

Another reason was the concern for the safety of the escapee. It was common knowledge that the Nazis would shoot any escaped prisoner, whether they were caught while trying to escape or if they would be recaptured. They felt as if it was too much to ask of a man to have him risk recapture when it would mean certain death at the hands of the Nazis.

There was also another reason why the Army made a practice of sending escaped prisoners home. The officials evidently had concerns about the mental makeup of a soldier after he had spent time in confinement. I guess there had been many documented incidents of the onset of many types of mental illnesses and such after a man goes through the trauma of being held prisoner. They just didn't think it was a good idea for a man of questionable mental capacities to be sent back into battle. Even if the escaped prisoner of war had managed to deal with his confinement from a mental illness standpoint, it still traditionally had some lasting effects on him. After a man knows what it's like being captured, then they will go to great lengths not to be recaptured, sometimes too great lengths. This could, in the right circumstances be a great detriment to the unit and put many men's lives in danger.

As far as I could tell, I was having no major lasting effects from my stay in the prisoner of war camp, at least that were too serious. I was beginning to have some continuing dreams, or maybe I should more appropriately say nightmares about my stay. I would sometimes wake up in a sweat thinking about the beatings I had endured and the way I felt during my stay with the Nazis. The nightmares that I was subject to became less and less frequent but were still occurring.

I really didn't feel as if I would be a detriment to my unit. I didn't think I would be overly cautious while going to too great lengths to avoid recapture. I guess, though, it would actually be very difficult to say how one would react until put into the situation itself.

When I first heard that I was going home, I was very happy. I was glad to get myself out of this. I had just spent quite a while being treated in an incredibly inhumane way during my stay in the prisoner of war camp. I didn't look forward to putting myself in a position to be taken prisoner again.

It felt pretty good to realize that I was actually going to survive this bloody conflict, especially with all I had been through. I knew that even though the war had seemed to turn in our direction and it looked more and more as if we would win the war, it was long from over. If I had to stay and go back into battle, I would be faced with more and more life-threatening situations. I thought that in the short time I had been in battle that I had already faced my share of near death experiences. I knew that I wouldn't have to face this any more if I got to go home. These aspects made me feel good about going home.

As good as these thoughts made me feel about going home, there were also some reasons that I would actually rather stay. First of all I felt very patriotic about my duty to my country. I wanted to help win the war. I felt very bad about going home while many others would have to stay here and put their lives in danger on a daily basis to help serve their country.

I also wanted to see the men of my unit again. I wanted them to know that I had made it back alive. Remember that I wasn't sure if they even knew that I was alive. In fact, I was pretty sure that they had no idea of whether I was alive or not. I wanted to see these men again, especially my buddy, Rose. I definitely wanted to see Rose again, at least to say goodbye.

I also didn't really feel like I had that much to go home to. My childhood had been very tough and I didn't see that being adult there would be much better. In some ways, I guess I knew that I was destined to fight battles in my life. I would just as soon fight them against the Nazis.

Even though I couldn't convince them to let me stay on active duty, I did make some headway. I convinced them to let me visit my unit for a few days before I was to head back to the states. I was very relieved that I would get to see the members of my unit, especially Rose. I couldn't wait to see him.

I was taken back to our unit. All the members of the unit greeted me very warmly. They were shocked to see me. They had not gotten any official word on me, but they had assumed that I must have been killed in action.

I finally saw my buddy. It seemed like forever since I had seen my dear friend. He was absolutely elated that I had made it back to the unit alive. I was equally as thrilled to see him.

We got a chance to take a few moments and catch up. Rose told me how he had gone over and over the circumstances surrounding my capture. He said that he had had a very difficult time dealing with my disappearance. He felt as if he might have done something wrong. He was afraid that he had somehow been the cause of my apparent downfall in that village. He said he kept thinking that I might have needed his backup and he was not there for me. Rose had struggled with a great feeling of guilt since that day that I had disappeared from the unit.

I made sure that my friend realized that there was absolutely nothing that he could have done to prevent my capture. He was only doing his duty by going back to our unit to report the situation in the village.

I tried to make him feel better, but as I thought more about it I understood the way he felt. Rose and I were the best of friends, which was something I had really never had the opportunity to have back home. We were very close, but it was more than that for the two of us.

Remember that Rose had been my number two scout. He was my back up, my support. We were each others support out there. When you put your life in the hands of someone day after day like the two of us had, you develop a bond more solid than most people have the opportunity to experience. We had gone out into battle after battle together with members of our unit. We had all developed a sense of closeness with all the men in our unit. This was magnified infinitely between someone like my buddy, Rose and I.

Even though I tried to comfort my friend, I understood where he was coming from. I knew this because if I were in his shoes I would have felt the same way. The two of us had developed a sense of responsibility for each other's safety. It was part of our duty, but it was even more than that. We had developed a bond that made us a great team in our scouting. I knew that if Rose felt the same way that I did, that he would rather not come back from a mission himself than to have me not make it back safely. He would later prove that he indeed did feel the same way.

I was given the opportunity to stay with the unit for a few days before I would be sent home. I relished this fact because it gave me the chance to catch up with the men of the unit, especially Rose.

I'm sure that most men in my situation would not have felt the same way. They most likely would have wasted no time trying to get out of there and head back home. I wouldn't blame them, but I sure didn't feel this way. I actually wanted to stay with the unit for a while.

I spent the next couple of days reacquainting myself with the members of the unit. Some of the guys were starting to make entertainment requests of me. They talked about how they missed me and my traveling show. I sang a little and told a few jokes, just acting silly in general. It was the first inkling of any kind of fun that I had had in a very long time.

I managed to spend a lot of time with Rose, too. The unit was not currently engaged in any kind of hostilities, so we were not as tight as we had been in certain circumstances. We had word that it appeared that things would most likely stay this way for a little while.

Even though we were not currently battling, we had to still take up regular precautions. Our unit had to be prepared in case something unexpected happened. One of these precautions was that I had to stay near the back of the lines. I did this so that my chances of being captured were very much minimized if some skirmish did breakout unexpectedly. This was a safety precaution that they employed for all recovered prisoners of war, but it still made me feel good.

Another aspect of my return to the unit that made me feel very good was the way the men reacted to me. They all realized the situation that I was in, and did their best to make sure that I stayed near the rear of the unit. It was a subtle way of showing that they cared about me.

This continued for a few days while I waited for my eventual return home. There were only certain times and situations in which I would have the opportunity to leave. While I was waiting for my call to head out, fate stepped in and changed my plans for going home.

The sound was suddenly deafening. It seemed to come out of nowhere. There was fire in the nighttime sky and the entire area was lit up like daylight. The quiet that had been present for the last several days was gone.

The Germans had mounted an offensive and we were caught somewhat off guard by it. Our unit scurried for cover. The fighting was fierce and there were heavy casualties in our unit. We were now struggling to get ourselves organized to deal with the severe blow and to mount a counter offensive.

I was in somewhat of a no man's land. I was not really prepared for battle. I had not even been issued a weapon. This was quickly dealt with as the Captain threw me a weapon for me to defend myself with. I suddenly found myself back in action as our unit was in the middle of a fierce battle with the Germans.

Because of this unexpected turn of events, my scheduled trip states side had been temporarily postponed. The vehicles and men that would be used to transport soldiers out had to be used for more important duties. I was stuck in battle with my unit, at least for the time being.

This was another instance in which my feelings at the time were probably different than most. As much as part of me wanted to get out of this and go home, I couldn't help but think that it was better for me to stay. It's hard to explain, but I really wanted to stay. As I said earlier, I really didn't have anything to hurry back to, and I didn't want to come home knowing that my buddies were still out here somewhere in the battlefield fighting for their country. As difficult as it may be to believe, I really was glad that I was staying with the unit.

The next few days were very rough. The Germans had caught us by surprise and it took us an extended time to regroup our forces and call for some support. After some days of fierce combat, we were finally able to hold our position and then move on the German unit.

The men in the unit continued to pay close attention to my whereabouts. They were now even more concerned about my safety as we dealt with the German offensive. I would look and notice someone close to me watching me very closely. I have to admit that it made me feel good. I felt honored that the men thought enough of me to risk their own lives to help look out for me. It sure made me feel important. To this day, I still get a warm feeling just thinking of their gesture.

I now found myself moving from a mode of thinking that I was on my way home to Southern Illinois to my battle mode. I started to think about the different aspects of our unit and its battle preparation. I started to wonder who our scout was. I then arrogantly started to ponder if I would do a better job in my old position.

I didn't wonder about this issue for very long before I decided to go to the Captain and volunteer for my old spot as number one scout. The Captain and some of the other men in the unit thought I was crazy. I guess they were probably right.

Chapter 18

Rose and I were a team again. We jumped right back into our old positions as if nothing had ever happened to keep us apart. I reassumed my position as number one scout and Rose was back at his familiar number two position. It really felt great to be back at my post.

I really can't say that my capture and eventual escape effected how I performed my duty. I knew that some men were never the same after spending time as a prisoner of war. I heard stories of men who were too fearful of recapture to be useful to their unit. I guess this was one of the reasons that most everyone was surprised at my eagerness to retake my position as number one scout.

Even though I seemed to have minimal lingering effects from my capture, I could certainly understand why some men would have difficulty dealing with it. It was indeed an intensely traumatic experience to have to live through. Don't get me wrong, even I didn't escape my experience in the German POW camp without any lasting effects, but they were minimal.

At the time, I used to have nightmares on a fairly regular basis. I used to dream that I was back inside the walls of the camp. I used to relive in those dreams the beatings that I had taken at the hands of the Nazis. It definitely wasn't very pleasant, but for whatever reason I seemed to be able to wake from those dreams and realize that it was over and I could move on.

I also probably was a little more cautious than I used to be before my capture by the Germans. I really can't say that I was overly cautious in my duty, but probably more careful than I had been before my stay in Germany. There was only a certain amount of caution that you could use as number one scout and also perform your duty effectively for the unit.

I was definitely one of the more fortunate man who spent time as a prisoner of war. I heard many stories of how men sometimes were not able to deal with the experience of spending time in captivity. I'm sure that many men were humiliated by the ordeal. Many men may have broken at the beatings and gave information to the Nazis. Even though I, myself was able to withstand the brutal beatings without giving any more information other than my name, rank, and serial number, I could definitely never blame anyone who did divulge any kind of information that the Nazis were looking for. They, as they say, "had ways of making you talk."

I also heard of situations in which the captive soldier would make deals to give information for favors. I had a much more difficult time respecting those men that decided to take this route. I understood that such incredibly desperate circumstances made men do things that they normally would never do, but it was hard to imagine not choosing death over selling out your country.

I guess it happened fairly regularly, though if information I was told was correct many more men withstood the beatings and interrogation without giving into the methods of torture. It was a great testament to the courage and patriotism of the many American, and also Allied troops who served in World War II. I was proud to just be associated with these men that I had the privilege to serve with.

As I mentioned, I was probably a little more cautious, but I can't say the same for my comrades. They weren't a little more cautious. They were a lot more cautious. They made it a priority to keep an eye on me. The entire unit kept a close watch on me while we were in battle.

The battles were very fierce there in Belgium in the early winter of 1944. We were a Reconnaissance Unit, which meant that in most every confrontation we usually found ourselves outnumbered by the enemy. It made it difficult for us to make progress into the German lines.

Some days we would stay put in one area all day, or sometimes even for days at a time. Many times our unit fought hard all day and made only a small amount of progress. Sometimes this was only a few yards, if not a few feet. Those few precious feet many times cost many lives.

In some instances we actually had to retreat from our position. We would be engaged in fierce battle in which we were outnumbered, sometimes incredibly so. Our unit had to work very hard not to be pushed back, let alone make a small amount of progress. It was a very tough period for us.

As difficult as the Germans made it for our progress, there was one thing that hindered our push through Belgium even more – the weather. We spent many very difficult days of fighting through very heavy rain. This hindered our efforts drastically. It hindered our visibility, which was crucial for our unit. It was especially tough on me as number one scout. I had to move ahead of the unit until I would spot the enemy, so that we would not be caught by surprise. The heavy rain made this very difficult for me to perform my duty effectively.

The rain also made it tough for our men as we were establishing our position in battle. The water created very muddy conditions that made it tough to move quickly and precisely. With all the wetness the troops of our unit had to make sure to keep their weapons dry and ready to fire at a moments notice.

Now lying in the middle of the Belgium countryside was not pleasant under the best of battle circumstances. This was multiplied significantly by the fact that we were, on these rainy days, lying in thick mud. Our clothes were soaked and this is the way we generally had to stay until nature, through dry weather conditions let them dry. This had to happen while we were wearing them. I'm sure you can imagine how uncomfortable this was for us.

The rain during the day would have been tough enough, but the nights were much worse. The area of Europe that we were now stationed in was notorious for their severely brutal winters. The winter of 1944 was not the normal winter for this part of the world, it was much more severe. The temperatures during the nighttime of the winter of 1944 were absolutely off the charts. The temperatures would fall as low as thirty to forty degrees below zero.

These brutal temperatures would have been difficult enough to deal with for a clean, dry, warmly dressed soldier, and we were none of those things. We were filthy from crawling around in the mud all day. We also were wet from the rains and sometimes snow during the day. We also were not dressed in the most appropriate winter gear for the conditions we found ourselves in.

It still makes me feel cold today just to think about it. The conditions were almost unbearable. Our uniforms would get wet during the day. The temperatures would then fall many degrees below zero at night.

Our uniforms would then literally freeze. They would actually freeze to our skin, which was also wet. I can remember staying in one place for a period of time and then not being able to move. Something was holding me back. I would investigate and find that my uniform had frozen to the ground.

It escapes me how in the world that all of us didn't end up with severe cases of frostbite. There were cases of frostbite, but I managed to avoid the condition, at least officially. I had felt all of the conditions of frostbite, though I was not diagnosed with the condition. I'm sure many cases of frostbite went undiagnosed. What I'm trying to say is that I most likely had frostbite, but was never actually officially told by a medic or doctor that I had it.

As you can probably understand by the conditions that I have described, we were faced with very difficult circumstances. It seemed as if we were not going to survive these brutal conditions. I'm sure you realize what kind of effect these conditions had on our morale.

I had been a part of many difficult situations in my service in the war up to this point, including Normandy and being taken as a prisoner of war. The morale of the men that I was with was at an all time low. It was pretty difficult to keep a positive attitude under these circumstances. It seemed to go on and on. We fought extremely hard, in unbearable conditions and seemed to make very little progress, if we made any progress at all. This opened the door for morale to take a severe dip, and ours did. Our will to carry on was definitely under the test.

It was definitely difficult to keep our spirits up. My biggest test of my will to carry on would come shortly thereafter. I would soon face the saddest experience of my life to that point.

We started that day as we had started many before. Rose, who was an extremely devout Christian and I, who was not a Christian at the time would get together for our prayer time before we headed out on our scouting duty. Rose's prayers always made me feel good. I felt that as important as this prayer time was for Rose, it had become equally important to me.

That particular day, Rose seemed even more sincere in his prayer than ever before. He always felt as if it were his Christian duty to pray for his fellow man. He prayed for me and for all the other members of our unit as we faced our battles. That day you could really feel the sweet spirit in the air, and as I stated earlier, I wasn't even a Christian at the time.

I started to feel as if God was, in fact, watching out for me. I started to question this fact a little after my capture and during my stay in the prisoner of war camp. Now, after making it through that brutal experience, I felt even more like God was looking out for me. I sure appreciated those daily prayers that Rose and I shared together. I didn't realize at the time though that my good buddy, Rose and I had just spent our last prayer time together.

As I got up from our prayer, I noticed that something seemed to be bothering Rose. He didn't seem like his usual self. Remember that we were going through a lot at the time with the battle conditions we were faced with, but it was more than that.

I asked Rose what was bothering him. He hesitated for a few moments. He didn't seem to want to talk to me about it. He then reluctantly opened up to me. He asked if in all the battle experience that we had had together, if I had ever got up in the morning feeling like I wouldn't make it through the day. I told him that the day I was captured seemed a little odd, maybe that something was gonna' happen, and happen it certainly did.

Rose then confided in me the feeling that he was having. He said he had this sinking feeling that he would not make it through the day. I quickly told him that he was crazy. I told him that someone like him would always find a way to make it. Even though I wasn't a Christian, I knew that God was definitely looking out for Rose. Surely he would be all right. Undoubtedly he would make it through the day.

I think Rose knew then what I eventually found out. I can't really explain it, and I guess neither can anyone else, but it seems that many people seem to know it when they are facing death. I've heard many stories about people making preparations as if they knew it was the end. I don't know exactly how it works, but I believe that sometimes the Lord gives you that feeling in advance to help you prepare.

I tried to shrug off Rose's comments. I tried to just forget it. I tried to ignore it and go on about my duty, but I couldn't. It was weighing very heavily on my mind as the two of us headed out to perform our duty, to be the scouts for our unit.

The two of us then headed out to scout for the enemy. I found myself thinking over and over about Rose's comment about not making it through the day. It caused me to pay particular close attention to my friend. I would look out for him. I would protect him. I would make sure that he made it through the day.

I made it to the usual distance ahead of the unit looking for the enemy. I crawled around in some brush area while looking for the enemy with one eye and trying to look out for Rose with the other.

Then up ahead in the distance I spotted something. I would soon make it to an area of trees where I had a much better view. It was the enemy. It was a German unit. They were situated there in Belgium near the German border. I signaled Rose to let him know and to get word to the unit.

I tried to get closer to get a better look at the Germans. It would give us a better idea of what we should do next. If it were a small unit, we might decide to try to take them now. If they were a very large unit, we might be better served to go around them, or even stay put until we got some back up.

I found what I believed to be a good spot along a row of trees. I then proceeded to watch the German unit, trying to get a better idea of what I should advise the unit to do next. It seemed as if I was hidden very well and that no one had spotted me from my position in the row of trees.

I waited there for a few minutes trying to gather as much information as I could. Then suddenly it happened. Suddenly out of nowhere I heard a noise. It wasn't an incredibly loud noise, in fact it was little more than the rustling of the grass. Then I saw it! It was a grenade – a live grenade!

I watched the grenade for a moment trying to get my mind to process exactly what I was seeing. Was it really a grenade? – A live grenade? That's exactly what it was and it was lying right in front of me.

It was a very surreal experience for me. Everything seemed to move into slow motion. I watched the grenade knowing that it would most certainly explode and do so very quickly. I had to get out of there, but realistically I knew that there was no time. There was absolutely not enough time for me to get away.

I couldn't help but think as I watched the grenade, that this was it. I had made it through so much, but there was no way I could make it through this. I had let my guard down once in that French village and it had cost me an extended stay in Germany. I had done it again and this time it was apparently going to cost me my life. The most important word is apparently.

As the events continued to seem to be in slow motion, I saw him. I saw him coming out of the corner of my eye. He was moving and moving fast. As I stayed there basically with my mouth hanging open, my friend Rose was by no means stationary. He moved toward me.

What was he doing? He had no time to get to me and push me out of the way. There simply wasn't time.

My buddy knew this. You see he had no thoughts of trying to push me out of the way. He knew that he never could do it in time. He did know, however, that he did have time for one thing. He had time to save my life.

My best friend in the world then jumped toward the grenade. What was he doing? He was saving me. He was doing the only thing he could do to save me. I then watched my best buddy throw himself on that live grenade.

I heard the explosion, but then again I didn't. I'm not sure I actually saw or heard anything for quite some time. That same explosion was fierce. Fire shot high into the air and the blast knocked me down. I got up after the explosion and tried to get my senses back.

I then quickly made my way over to the area where I saw my best friend lying. I was yelling his name – Rose! It seemed to take forever to get to him. He was not moving as he lied there in the Belgium countryside near the German border.

When I finally got to my friend I turned him over to see the absolute horror of what a grenade can do to the human body. His abdominal area was completely ravaged. Blood was pouring everywhere. His insides were no longer that, as his organs were exposed. It was an incredibly horrible sight. It was easy to see instantly that Rose's wounds had been fatal.

I held my best friend on the battlefield that day as he lay dead in my arms. He had been right. He had not made it through the day. He was gone. He would never go home again. He would never see his parents who most assuredly would be devastated. He would never get the chance to marry and raise a family. He would never get the opportunity to do all the things that boys of that tender young age should be looking forward to doing.

My best friend had given it all. He had sacrificed it all, and he had done it for me. He had given his life to save mine. I couldn't help but notice his face. I looked into that face and saw a very sweet smile, a very peaceful smile, and seemingly a very happy smile. It was almost as if he had been smiling when he died. It was if he was actually happy about what he was prepared to do.

I truly believe that he was happy. Later while familiarizing myself with scripture, I read in the Bible "Greater love hath no man than this that a man lay down his life for his friends." - John 15:13.

Rose not only lived by the Bible, but he died by it also. It was a great testimony, one that would have an incredible impact on my life. I would now, however, have to face life without the best friend I ever had.

Chapter 19

To say that I was devastated seems too mild in describing my feelings after watching my best friend die while saving my life. I was absolutely crushed. I felt like I just could not go on. I had seen a lot of death on the battlefields as we made our way across Western Europe, but nothing like this. I had always managed to deal with death before. I was always able to deal with it and move on. It was almost like it really didn't happen. I guess I just didn't dwell on it.

Maybe that was my way of dealing with the heartache of the numerous deaths we were witness to on a daily basis. Maybe it was the only way for my psyche to deal with the pain and not totally lose my mind. I wasn't really sure of the reasons why I had been able to put aside the killing up to this point, all I knew was that it was now all rushing in at once.

I had not had such a feeling of utter remorse since the death of my grandfather when I was six years old. I sure missed him terribly for what seemed to be the longest of time. After a while though, the pain seemed to ease and the pain of remembering my grandfather became cherished memories.

I knew it was now just after the fact, but it didn't feel as if I would ever get to that point in dealing with the death of Rose. With grandpa I was really too young to even understand the circumstances of his apparent murder, I just knew that he was gone and I missed him a lot. With Rose, I knew the circumstances of his death all too well. He had died to save me. He had given his life to preserve mine.

At the time I'm not sure that I realized it, but I was absolutely mired in guilt. I kept replaying the circumstances surrounding Rose's act of heroism over and over in my head. I kept reliving it again and again. Like we sometimes tend to do when something tragic happens, I kept analyzing the tragedy over and over, hoping I could figure out how I could possibly have done something differently, as if I would get a chance to do it all over again.

I went over and over my behavior on that day. I started doing the "What if…?" routine. What if I hadn't tried to get closer to that German unit? What if I had been paying closer attention and had seen the German throw the grenade? What if Rose had been just a split second late in returning from notifying the unit? What if the grenade had exploded before Rose had a chance to cover it and save me? What if…? What if…? What if…?

I did get some consolation in some of my thoughts about the incident. I got great pleasure knowing that I had the opportunity to even meet Rose. Fate had brought us together via World War II. Had it not been for the global conflict, the two of us would never had the opportunity to meet. As I said, I had never really had a close friend back home. I was always too busy helping around the house to develop any lasting friendships. I had definitely had that with Rose.

I thought a lot about just what Rose's act meant to me. I could hardly imagine the incredible love that he must have had for me to do what he did. I was more sorry than I can even begin to explain about the fact that Rose had died, but on the other hand, Rose's act of amazing kindness made me feel incredibly good inside. It would have a huge impact on my life in too many ways to list.

I also found myself contemplating what Rose and I had discussed after our prayer that morning. He said he had this feeling that he wasn't going to make it through the day. At the time I figured he was probably just feeling depressed at the thought of the circumstances that our unit was facing out here on the battlefield. I thought that the conditions might be catching up with him. This just wasn't like him. He was always so content with life even in the most difficult of circumstances, but he was more serious on this day.

I wondered if Rose had actually been given a direct message from God. Did he really know he was going to die that day? Did he know that he was going to have to sacrifice his life for mine? I didn't know the answers to these thought-provoking questions, but I pondered them in my mind.

Rose had been my first real witness about Jesus. I had heard about Christ from people back home, but I never had any long-term exposure to Christians because my family didn't attend church services. It made me contemplate my own bout with eternity for the first time.

I found myself wondering about Rose's sincere devotion to God and what that had meant to him as he lived his life. He always seemed content even when he wasn't happy. He seemed to possess a peace that was beyond understanding. I didn't quite understand what that peace was, but what I did know is that I wanted it.

Rose was a person that you could just see love in. He was kind, gentle, and compassionate toward others. He witnessed to all of us about Christ. He felt like it was his Christian duty. When he talked to us, I could just feel how much he sincerely wanted us to be saved. Saved to me then was a physical kind of save, as in saving someone from being blown up by a grenade.

The kind of save that Rose spoke of was different. It was a spiritual save. It meant that your soul was saved for eternity. It meant eternity in Heaven. As I mentioned, I wasn't quite sure about all the details, but I knew what Christ had done for Rose's life and I knew I wanted him to do that in mine.

I continued to often think of Rose. I found myself fighting with more passion than ever before. I guess I was trying to avenge the death of my friend. If I shot someone, I said this is for you, Rose. It made me feel better momentarily, but I later learned that you can never avenge violence with more violence.

As the battles continued to rage in early December of 1944, I found myself feeling very lonely as I faced each day of combat. I had no word of what was going on back home with my family. I had found out that there was no official word of any bombings in the contiguous United States as the German guards had told me. As I mentioned earlier, I didn't necessarily believe them, but I did not rule it out either. I had heard stories of the German submarines off the Atlantic coast and also heard tell that the Japanese had actually flown planes over California. Neither of these had been confirmed, but there was talk.

Franklin D. Roosevelt was still in command of our forces. He had in early November just been elected to an unprecedented fourth term as President of the United States. In fact, he had been the only man to serve three terms, let alone four. Other than major things like that we didn't get much word of news back home. I felt isolated and very alone.

Our push toward the German border had become somewhat stalled in the hilly and wooded, Ardennes country, as we neared the Nazi homeland. I believe that high-ranking officials realized that our morale was very low out on the Belgium battlefield. I'm sure they tried to come up with ways to bolster our morale out there.

A rumor started to float around that we would be served turkey on Christmas Day. Now that was a couple of weeks away, but you probably can't imagine what a stir that news caused in our unit. We had been fed pretty well in comparison to my stay in the prisoner of war camp, but the food was definitely nothing to write home about. The news that we were set to feast on half a turkey each, made our mouths water just at the thought of the bird.

We hoped it was true, but we didn't bank on it. We did know, however, that we had managed to outrun our supplies. We were desperately low on everything from food to ammunition. We knew that we would certainly have to get some kind of shipment of supplies and get them soon, or we were in trouble. We all hoped that included in this shipment would be the turkey. We hoped for something that ultimately would never come.

Things continued on in about the same pattern until the morning of December 16, 1944. On that day the Germans launched a major offensive against our forces there in Western Europe. We were caught by surprise by the incredibly risky move on the part of the Nazis. This day was to signal the beginning of the German Ardennes Offensive, or as it became better known the Battle of the Bulge.

The Ardennes is a region of wooded plateaus and rounded peaks. This area is a very important part of the world in historical realms. It had been a major battle ground in World War I and would prove to be the same in World War II. Its proximity to major corridors of Western Europe has proved to make it an extremely popular battleground through the years.

The German offensive consisted of sending in a wave of approximately a quarter of a million troops to hit the center of the Allied front in Western Europe. The Nazi strategy was based on catching the Allies off guard by their daring move, which they most certainly did. The Germans were thought to be on their last leg and the last thing the Allies thought was that they would mount a major offensive, but that's exactly what they did.

We learned later that Hitler himself had endorsed the strategy. He had been advised by some of his officials that it could never work, but he was determined to proceed anyway. Some people have speculated that Hitler at this time may have gone over the edge mentally, as if he hadn't already.

The crux of the plan consisted of the Germans hitting the Allies in the middle of their front in Western Europe, thereby dividing the Americans. Their goal was to take back the major city of Antwerp.

The strategy was most effective initially. As I said, we were caught by surprise by the attack. Our casualties were heavy. The Germans under the direction of generals Gerd von Rundstedt and Hasso von Manteuffel actually advanced into Allied lines. They cut deeply into established American lines for about eight days. Their advance had gone approximately 50 kilometers or about 31 miles into Belgium and Luxembourg. They had successfully created a "bulge" hence the name of the battle.

The fighting was the fiercest of the war. A Nazi unit that outnumbered us at least two to one overran our unit. We were in full retreat. Our men were scurrying for cover. Our casualties were extremely heavy. In our retreat I faced yet another instance of knowing that someone was watching over me.

The shells were blasting on all sides of me. It seemed even denser that it had been at Normandy, if that indeed is possible. I was literally running for my life. I could feel the Germans almost literally breathing down my collar. I then saw a foxhole filled with Americans. I decide to join them to avoid the fire.

I jumped into the midst of the men. There was several of them lying very still in that foxhole. They reminded me of the way the Germans were lying in that unit I ran across while I was on the run after my escape from the prisoner of war camp. They reminded me of them for good reason. The Americans in the foxhole that I had found myself in were also all dead.

I could hear the German troops approaching. I knew that I had no time to leave the foxhole to try to escape. They were much too close. It would be suicide. I decided that my only option was to try to play dead amongst the fallen Americans that were there with me.

I then lay very still and tried to cover myself as much as I could by the bodies of the men in the foxhole. I tried not to breathe which was particularly difficult under the circumstances. I had been running at full speed to get away from the Germans, had jumped into this foxhole, and was more nervous at the prospect of what I was facing than you can even imagine. A German soldier then made it to our foxhole. He looked around and saw that the men were dead. I thought for a moment that he might just move on assuming that we were all dead, no such luck.

The Nazi then paused and readied his rifle. He then proceeded to fire several rounds into the foxhole. I guess he wanted to make sure there were no surviving soldiers in that foxhole. He did just that, with one exception that is.

I couldn't believe it, but not one of those shells that the Nazi soldier fired into that foxhole hit me anywhere. The German then moved on and advanced further into our lines along with many of his comrades. I waited for several minutes until I was sure the coast was clear. I continued to examine myself, still in shock that none of those shells had hit me. I then jumped up out of the foxhole and headed off into the wooded area for cover until I could find what was left, if there was anything left, of my unit.

I eventually hooked up with the remains of our unit. Our losses were heavy. We found an area in which we could establish ourselves and wait for reinforcements. That's where I witnessed one of the most horrific of the many inhumane acts on the part of the Nazis during the war.

We had managed to get to a place of cover in which we felt a certain degree of safety. From this position we could see the Nazis continue to advance through out lines. On their advance through our incredibly outnumbered units, the Germans managed to bring in many prisoners.

The Germans were having the captured men line up with their hands over their head. We believed that they were going to march them to some holding area before their apparent transport to some prisoner of war camp.

A group of Nazis with rifles then approached the men who had been captured. They then proceeded to fire toward the prisoners. They gunned them down! They actually fired on those defenseless men. I was absolutely shocked. I once again was horrified by the incredible inhumane atrocities on the part of the Nazis. It was a brutal act of cruelty beyond description. It was later dubbed as the "Malmedy Massacre", after the Belgium town near the German border close to where the killings took place. It was an act of sheer inhumanity in which 81 prisoners were murdered.

The battle appeared to be going heavily in the favor of the Nazis. It seemed that their strategy was working and they were well on their way to dividing us and even taking back Antwerp. It seemed that way until December 23.

Christmas was still two days away, but the Allies were given a much-needed present a little early. On December 23 the skies cleared.

This was of great significance to the Allied war effort. This clearing let the Allied planes get in the air for the first time since the Germans launched their major offensive. We had established our air superiority, but had not had a chance to take advantage of it because of the lack of visibility throughout the area.

This gift from nature soon signaled the end for the German offensive. Our planes were able to fly and bombard the German units. The tide quickly changed. The Germans were now in full retreat as they tried to make it back to their lines. The Germans had tried a last ditch effort to win the war and it had failed miserably.

The German Ardennes Offensive was very effective for a limited time. The German advance had gone well into Allied established lines. It actually took until the end of January of 1945 before the entire "bulge" was eliminated and the Allied advance into Germany really didn't proceed until February.

The Battle of the Bulge was extremely costly to the Nazis and their war effort. Even though it got off to a strong beginning, it ultimately was doomed by good weather that let Allied planes get into the air. Casualties were extremely heavy on both sides, but the Germans lost approximately 220,000 men in their ill-fated offensive.

The Battle of the Bulge was the largest land battle of World War II. The number of casualties was startling. Had the Germans been able to successfully divide the Americans with their surprise attack, things could have turned in favor of the Nazis. If they had been able to retake Antwerp and establish themselves there, it would have at least prolonged the war for probably many months. What it ended up being was the last offensive on the part of the Third Reich.

Chapter 20

Christmas, what a joyous season it is! It's a time for spending precious moments with family and friends. It's a time for exchanging gifts, singing carols, and most importantly, celebrating the birth of Jesus Christ. It's a time that many children look forward to all year.

Christmas Eve is a very special night. Most families are gathered together spending time with one another. Anxious children all over the world are overflowing with anticipation at the thought of the goodies that they would find under the tree the next morning. Women were busy planning and beginning preparations of magnificent Christmas dinners. This is the way most people spend their Christmas Eve. I was not so fortunate. I spent Christmas Eve of 1944 in Belgium near the German border on guard duty.

Being so very far away from home is almost never easy. Even though I didn't have the most desirable childhood, I still found myself homesick at certain times more than others. This was one time that I was really feeling it. I was wondering about what my family was doing on this day before Christmas. I wondered if the kids were having trouble sleeping like many children do as they anticipate what gift would be waiting for them the next morning.

These thoughts were running through my head as I performed my guard duty that day. It made it very difficult to concentrate on what I was doing. I tried not to think about things too much, but it was difficult. It was indeed a very emotional time for me and I believe for many of the men of our unit.

Christmas Day was a significant day in the course of World War II. Adolph Hitler had promised earlier that his German army would retake Paris and he had predicted that they would be back there by Christmas Day of 1944. Christmas was still a day away, but the German army was far from Paris and showed no signs of advancement let alone making it all the way back to the French capital.

The men in our unit had also been looking forward to Christmas time because of another promise. It was a promise made to us about a certain meal we were to partake in. The turkey dinner was widely anticipated by that group of hungry soldiers fighting through Belgium that Christmas season. The meal of turkey that we had been told we would be having never came. I have to admit as much as I wanted that meal that we had been promised, I really was not the least bit surprised that we didn't get it. We barely had enough of our regular supplies like ammunition. I really didn't anticipate getting any extras.

Christmas Day was also important because of its significance in battle. Traditionally battle is halted for Christmas Day. I was told that was true in World War I and that it would most likely be observed again in our fighting. The next day I witnessed that to be true, as our unit saw no signs of any kind of battles going on at least in our general vicinity.

Christmas Day did spell a halt in the fighting, at least for the day. That was very good news, but there was one negative thing about it. It gave us time to think about the situation we were in and how difficult it was for all of us to be away from home at this time of year.

The Germans took advantage of the season and the emotions of the soldiers who were away from home to use some of their propaganda techniques. They spread their propaganda to us Americans and other Allied troops by radio. The most famous of their radio broadcasters was "Axis Sally."

She called herself "Midge at the mike", but the troops knew her as "Axis Sally." She hosted a program called "Home Sweet Home." It was a German program filled with Nazi propaganda that was heard throughout Europe. It was mainly broadcast for our ears as we spent time in Western Europe making our way toward Germany. Its goal was to dampen our spirits and take a shot at lowering our already dwindling moral to lessen our will to fight.

Sally had a very sexy and sultry voice. Much like her Southwest Pacific counterpart, "Tokyo Rose", "Axis Sally" liked to tease and taunt soldiers about their love lives. She liked to talk about how their wives and girlfriends must be very lonely back home in the United States. She would always try to work in some comment to the effect of insinuating that their wife or girlfriend is more than likely taking up with the 4Fs back home in America.

The Nazis hope was to take our minds off of fighting by giving us something to think about. They also hoped to dash our will to fight on. They correctly figured that a man that was too worried about an unfaithful wife or girlfriend did not make for a very effective soldier.

The Germans were definitely good at their trade. They were well aware of the things that war brought to the lives of couples. It was a difficult situation to be in. These couples were many miles apart for an extended time period. I heard a lot of stories of men in our unit receiving the classic "Dear John" letters. Many lonely women had turned to men who were there at hand. They shared their affections with someone that was there for them, sometimes while their husband or boyfriend was stuck fighting for his life on a battlefield somewhere. The Germans took this very unfortunate aspect of war and ran with it.

Sally would get the names and serial numbers of captured GIs. I later learned that she would many times go to the men and pass herself off as a Red Cross worker. She would then get the captured and sometimes injured soldier to record a message for her to supposedly send back home to their worried families to let them know that they were all right. They would indeed broadcast the messages back to the United States, but they definitely had ulterior motives.

The Nazis would then use this recorded message as propaganda. Sally would take the message recorded by the imprisoned soldier and make some adjustments to it. She would lace the message with Nazi propaganda that was intended to make soldiers on the battlefield and families back home question the direction that our leaders were going in the execution of wartime strategy.

We listened to Sally on many occasions. She evidently viewed how the war was going the same way that the guards in the prisoner of war camp did. She used to talk about how Germany was winning battle after battle. She told us that the war was just about to come to an end and that the Third Reich would be victorious.

She would also talk, as the guards in the prisoner of war camp did, that the Germans had successfully bombed many major cities. I have to admit that when I was in the camp I did sometimes wonder if what the guards were telling me about the war and about cities back home being destroyed was true. They now had a much more difficult time convincing me of this while I could see what we were doing on the battlefield. We didn't get news of the happenings on the battle fronts and back home on a daily basis, but there was definitely no indication that these things were true.

I listened to "Axis Sally" as she broadcast her show on Christmas of 1944. She was in rare form as far as spreading her Nazi propaganda. I remember her talking about how our government had sent us over to trespass on their territory this Christmas instead of being home with our families where we should be. She took many shots at our President and the leaders of the Allied countries for doing this to us.

I had always listened to the propaganda and really hadn't been too affected by it. We had been warned of the material that we would hear and that we should pay no attention to it. I had never let any of the things that were said by Sally or any of the Nazis during their broadcasts get to me, that is until Christmas of 1944.

As I mentioned earlier, I had done some singing to help entertain the guys during long days of intense waiting. This usually helped loosen them up a little. I was a bit of a country and western music fan. My favorite country and western singer was a man by the name of Earnest Tubbs. He had many songs that I listened to as I was growing up back home.

After talking about how difficult it must be for us soldiers to be away from home, "Axis Sally" finally managed to put something over the airwaves that got to me. She played "I'll Be Home For Christmas" by Earnest Tubbs. I became very emotional. I just couldn't hold back the tears. I cried like a baby that day as I listened in.

After the war ended, I found out that "Axis Sally's" real name was Mildred Gillars. She amazingly enough was an American, born in Portland, Maine. She reportedly had wanted to be an actress and ended up going to Europe. After spending some time in France, she then went to Germany in 1935. She became an English instructor in Berlin, but because of a relationship with a radio executive, took a job with Radio Berlin, as an announcer and actress. I absolutely couldn't believe that it was actually an American who had been spreading all that anti-American propaganda.

Mildred Gillars was brought to trial for war crimes after the war ended. She eventually was convicted of a count of treason for her exploits on German radio. She had become one of the most widely known names in the annals of World War II.

With the clearing on December 23, the tide turned in the Battle of the Bulge. We now had been able to reestablish ourselves with the massive air support. Even though things were going better for us, it was still a very difficult time for each of us.

Depression and fatigue were taking their toll on us. We now had been battling fiercely for an extended time period. We were extremely tired. We fought all day in some of the heaviest combat of the war and we also sometimes fought all night depending on the specific circumstances of the battle that we found ourselves in. We were not completely without food, but we were all hungry. Our nutrition level had to be getting close to a danger zone physically. We were also cold after braving the brutal winter conditions for an extended period of time. It was very taxing on us all.

The intense physical conditions along with our very fragile mental state of mind opened the door for many types of emotional related conditions that stemmed from lack of food, sleep, and severe emotional trauma. While we were still in Belgium and making our way up to the German border, I witnessed three separate cases of what we commonly referred to as "shell shock."

"Shell Shock" is an old army term. It refers to a condition in which the soldier just emotionally snaps in the midst of battle conditions. It manifests itself in many ways. Sometimes the soldier will simply have a nervous breakdown. They might just cease to function normally mentally.

You could sometimes see it coming. You could see the glazed look in their eyes as if they see you, but yet they don't. They seemed to have their mind on something else other than the situation at hand. The man going through "shell shock" would sometimes get a crazed look on his face. It would seem then that somehow the soldier would just loose touch with reality.

The three cases that I witnessed all happened one right after another as we approached the German border. We had been in an area for an extended time period and had been shelled all day and all night. It was a horrible battle. Our casualties in our unit were very heavy. Many men were in foxholes that were blown to bits as their comrades watched in horror.

It was a very difficult confrontation because it seemed, as it does in many battles, that there was really no rhyme or reason as to who was unfortunate enough to be killed and who would get the chance to live to fight another day. It was kind of like playing Russian roulette. When you heard an incoming shell, you knew it could very well be headed for you. It was a very helpless feeling.

I don't pretend to know what these men who experienced "shell shock" were thinking, but I do know that they were under more mental trauma than a human should be exposed to. They saw their friends and fellow soldiers being killed in droves and this was their reaction to the horror.

The first soldier stood up out of his foxhole and just started running as fast as he could right toward the enemy lines. He was screaming very loudly and was firing his weapon as fast as he possibly could, really in no particular direction. He was very quickly gunned down.

In a very short time period two more of the soldiers in our unit followed suit. They did the same thing. They each stood up and then started running toward the enemy lines at a sprint. The Germans also very quickly gunned them down, like the first soldier before them.

I am by no means any kind of psychiatrist so I won't try to over-analyze the emotional state of these men. I do know that the human mind is a very fragile thing. I guess these men had just seen all the death and destruction that their minds would permit them to process. They just snapped. They couldn't take it any more. I heard other stories of "shell shock", but these were the only three that I witnessed and they happened only moments apart.

Really as I think back on the things that we as troops in World War II had to witness, all the killing and mass destruction, it's probably amazing that more men didn't have emotional breakdowns. It's just another example of the dedicated fighting spirit and mental toughness of the Americans and the Allies that fought in World War II.

Chapter 21

We continued to advance further into what was once German held areas of Belgium. We were nearing the Siegfried Line, which was the German-Belgium border. The Germans continued to fight very fiercely, but we continued to make our way into their ranks. On a good day our unit sometimes went as far as fifty miles into the once German held ground.

The attempt at splitting us in the Battle of the Bulge had not only failed miserably, but it had also cost the Germans dearly. They lost an incredible number of men in their last ditch effort at holding us off. Had it been successful, it would have been a very sound plan of attack, though fortunately for us it was not.

The Nazi regime appeared to be crumbling around them. They had more problems than just the American and Allied advancement on the western front. They also had to deal with the Soviets on the eastern front. During the first four months of 1945 a two-fold allied trap that was closing in on them was quickly hemming in the Germans.

On January 12, 1945, the Russians launched a tremendous assault on the eastern front. They had broken through the German lines and were making a push through the countries that Germany had steamed rolled through several months earlier.

In all of five days the Soviets made its way into Poland and had taken back Warsaw. It took them two days later to capture the Polish city of Krakow. The Nazis had lost their stronghold of Poland.

In the midst of the Soviets move in the east, on January 16, 1945, the first and third armies linked back up after being split during the initial moments of the Battle of the Bulge. The "bulge" that the Germans had created was officially gone from the Allied ranks.

The Nazis had been notorious for their extremely inhumane battle tactics. I had witnessed and been subject to them in many circumstances. I really only thought I understood just how inhumane the Nazis could be. We would soon start to get word of an atrocity of overwhelming proportions.

As they were making their way through Poland and Eastern Europe, the Soviets had come upon a prison camp that had been set up at Auschwitz – the now infamous Auschwitz. While the Russians explored the camp, they uncovered utter cruelty that would rival any of the history of this planet.

On January 26, the Russians were on their move through Poland and came upon the town of Auschwitz, which was located in southern Poland about thirty-two miles southwest of Krakow. They then proceeded to liberate the huge concentration camp that had been set up there.

Auschwitz was the largest of many concentration camps that Hitler and the Nazis had set up across Europe. These camps were set up to help annihilate the Jewish race. Jews were not the only group of people who were put to death in these camps. There were also Poles, Gypsies, and Soviet prisoners of war, but the people killed were predominantly Jews.

Hitler had a great hatred for the Jews. He had held his views of anti-Semitism since very early in his life. For some strange reasons Hitler had evidently blamed the Jewish people for just about every ill in society.

Hitler proceeded with his plans of genocide for the Jewish race by setting up these camps. The people sent to these camps were usually either killed almost instantly, usually by poisonous gas, used as slave labor in brutal conditions, or some were used for some types of medical tests.

We would only learn after the war the actual unfathomable statistics of the mass murder at the hands of the Nazis. Although no accurate records were kept, at Auschwitz alone the number of executions was estimated to be anywhere from 1.5 to 4 million. The Camp Commandant, Rudolf Hoss admitted later to at least 2.5 million deaths. Whatever the exact figure, approximately one-third of the five to six million Jews who were executed during World War II, died at Auschwitz.

We knew very little about these events as our unit made its way toward the German border. You have to give the German Army a certain amount of credit. They continued to fight with all they had. They made nothing easy for us as we continued our push toward the border.

Our unit finally made it to the Siegfried Line in mid-January of 1945. We had already gotten news that American units had already crossed over the German border and were meeting much resistance as they pushed inside the German borders.

Being the number one scout, I was naturally the first man from our unit to cross into Germany. I have to admit that it felt good to think that we were getting that close to what I believed at the time to be victory, but as I said, the Germans by no means were through fighting.

Just on the German side of the Siegfried Line, our unit found ourselves engaged in very heavy combat. The Germans seemed to be fighting with even more vigor. The German army may have been more motivated by the fact that the battles were now taking place on German soil. For the first time in the entire war, there was intense fighting inside the German borders.

The war was basically initiated by the Germans aggressions into Eastern Europe. While steam rolling through this area and taking possession of several smaller countries by force, all the battles were being fought on foreign soil, at least to the Germans. They had yet to feel the destruction from land battle after land battle. The Germans had taken several hits by American and British bombing raids, but there had been no land battles to speak of inside the German border.

The Germans were now fighting for their country's very existence, at least in the way they knew it then. They were fighting for their honor and their backs were against the wall. They sure came out fighting. During the battles inside the German border I found that out for myself.

I was up ahead of the unit in my position as number one scout. I had made contact with the enemy. They were in the area and I was in the process of getting word back to the unit of their position. I had thought that I had monitored the German unit without being seen. I found out in just a few moments just how very wrong that I was in my thinking.

As I was holding my position waiting for my unit to progress to engage the German unit, I heard a noise. It sounded very familiar, but I wasn't sure what it was. Then as I processed the sound in my head, I realized what the sound was. It was a sound that was very familiar to me.

Click.

That was the sound. It was a familiar click. It was the click of a rifle that had not gone off for some reason. I wondered where the click could have come from. I knew that none of the members of my unit had made it into the area yet. That meant that it had to come from an enemy rifle.

I then looked off into the distance and still didn't see anything. I then moved a tree branch and there he was. I found myself looking down the barrel of a rifle that was being held by a German. He had me square in his sights.

It was another one of those moments in which time seemed to freeze momentarily and then the next few moments seemed to happen in slow motion. I still wasn't sure if this was really happening. I could only stand there and stare at the German who was in the process of trying to gun me down.

One would think that your first reaction in that situation would be to run, or get down. You would have thought that I would have tried to do something to defend myself, to fight back, or at least get out of there. I did none of those things. I should have, but for some reason I just stood there.

I looked into his eyes as he looked into mine. I'm sure he saw the fear in my eyes as I saw the surprise in his. Usually on the battlefield we didn't get to see the enemy up close. I had had a few incidents of hand to hand combat, but it was very infrequent. I still continued to just stare.

The Nazi's weapon would not fire. He had me right where he wanted me and his weapon would not fire. I'm not sure whether his rifle was out of ammunition, or was jammed, all I knew was that for some reason there was no bullet heading my way. There should have been, but for some strange reason there was not. At least I didn't think so.

Then I wondered as I continued to live the moment in slow motion. Maybe I was shot. Maybe I just hadn't felt it yet. Had the pain been so devastating that it had numbed by body to the point that I could feel nothing? I wasn't sure of that. I wasn't sure of anything at that moment.

After struggling with the rifle for a few brief moments, the German finally threw the rifle down to the ground. There was my break. What a stroke of luck! I decided later on that there was a lot more than luck involved. That was my chance to get away. That's what I should do, get away and fast. Guess what I did. I stood right there continuing to gaze at the German.

I'm sure that the Nazi thought that I must be a crazy American for not firing back, or getting out of there. If that's what he thought he would have been right. I think that I was crazy at least for a split second. I'm not sure what caused me to freeze. Maybe it was the surprise of seeing the German there zeroed in on me. Maybe it was the extreme fear I was feeling at the thought of looking down the barrel of a rifle that was held by the German. Whatever it was I knew that I was fortunate that I was not lying on the ground full of holes.

The odd thing about the confrontation with the German was that just as I seemed to be awed by the situation, so did the Nazi. He tried to fire a few times before throwing down his rifle, but I was still standing there. The Nazi didn't seem to know what to do.

The German then got himself together and reached down and picked up a Lugar pistol. He then proceeded to point the pistol at me. I had been fortunate once, but this was the end. I had survived looking down the barrel of a rifle, but the German now had a pistol and it was pointing directly at me. I then heard another sound. It was again a very familiar sound. It was in fact very familiar, so familiar that I had just heard it only seconds ago.

Click.

There was that familiar sound. It couldn't be. It absolutely couldn't be. It couldn't be, but it was. It was really happening again. It was difficult to believe, but the German's Lugar pistol would not fire.

I know what you are probably thinking. Isn't this book supposed to be non-fiction? I don't blame you. If we were making this into a movie, the Hollywood producers would never even think about putting something like this in. They would say that it just would not be even remotely believable. I suppose that they'd be right in saying that. I guess it just goes to show you how true the old saying is about the truth being stranger than fiction.

I don't know how common it is for a weapon not to fire. I don't have any statistics on this. I suppose there probably aren't any statistics kept. I do know that in all the times I had worked with weaponry, it had happened only a couple of times. I'm not sure what the odds are of someone facing a gun in battle that would not fire for some reason, but I imagine that it must be very infrequent. I can't even begin to approach what the odds would be that someone would face two straight weapons that would not fire for some reason. The chances of this happening would be most astronomical, almost non-existent, but that's precisely what happened.

As I looked into the eyes of the now very frightened German, I almost felt sorry for the man. He had actually done a very good job of soldiering. He had managed to approach me without being seen and zero in on me. He had me dead to right. If his rifle had fired he would have probably blown me away before I even realized just exactly what had happened. Even after his rifle had misfired for whatever reason he still had the situation under control as he grabbed his pistol, but amazingly enough it wouldn't fire either. After going through all that, you had to feel for the poor guy. Yeah, I almost felt sorry for him – almost.

Now I may be slow in reacting to a situation like this, but give me a couple of misfiring weapons and I'll eventually decide that it might be a good idea to defend myself in some way or another. I finally came to my senses after seeing something that I had a hard time believing.

I regrouped and grabbed my weapon. I then proceeded to fire several shots into the German. He fell back and I got down and headed for cover knowing that the shots would bring more enemy troops to the area.

When I finally got myself to a place of reasonable cover and was eventually joined by my unit, I couldn't help but focus on what had just happened. The fact that I was actually alive was nothing short of a miracle. There was no earthly way that what had just happened should happen. I again found myself with the same feeling that someone was watching out for me. Wouldn't you argue with me after that?

We then continued the battles in the area near the German border. It was still very fierce, but we had been very successful. We had made a lot of headway. We had pushed further into Germany and were showing no signs of slowing down in our pursuit of victory.

We had taken many prisoners in our battles over the last few days. It was very tempting to treat the German prisoners of war in the same manner that I was treated or the way we had witnessed the Germans treat that group of unarmed prisoners out in the battlefield. As much as we would have liked to brutalize the Germans that we captured, we resisted the urge.

I later was in an area in which several German troops were surrendering to us. The men of our unit were taking them in. They secured their weapons and were walking them to the holding area to wait to be processed and taken in. I found myself looking at the individuals in that line up.

I knew that we were just doing our jobs and that this was the way war was fought. I knew that these men were the enemy and all the brutal things that the Nazis had done to our troops and to me personally. As I watched the faces of the men as they held their hands over their heads, they really didn't look like Nazis. They just looked like young men, men that were scared to death. I guess when you spend time yourself in an enemy prisoner of war camp it gives you more of an insight into what prisoners were thinking at the moment they were captured. It made me feel a little better to think that these men would be treated humanely, which was more than I could say for the way the Nazis, treated their prisoners.

As I watched the men being brought in I saw a sight that made me gasp. Could it be? Yeah, it was him. I'd know him anywhere. It was the German that I had stared down in battle, the one that should have been able to kill me on the spot, but was struck with the misfortune of having defective weaponry.

I looked at him for an extended time. I wondered who he was. I wondered if he had a family back in Germany. Did he have parents that were anxiously awaiting his return? I wondered if he had a girl waiting for him back home. I wondered what he had done for a living before being called to serve the Nazi regime.

I started to think about how different things could have been. I thought about how men's lives, a battle victory, and even the outcome of the entire war could hinge on such small items. I thought about how things would have been so much different if only that German's gun would have fired. I would probably be lying dead on the battlefield. The German would probably not be a prisoner of war and he more than likely would not have massive injuries to his chest area, injuries that I had inflicted.

I watched the German being loaded onto a stretcher. He appeared to be severely injured. I really thought that I probably had killed him on the spot. I caught him in the torso area with several shots. These were wounds than in my opinion would more than likely be fatal, but there he was still alive.

In contrast to the brutal treatment that our prisoners of war received at the hands of the Nazis, our prisoners were treated more than fairly. One unofficial custom that the men used to do was to give cigarettes to enemy soldiers that were injured. It was an act of kindness usually reserved for prisoners with severe injuries, usually potentially fatal wounds.

The German that I had met on the battlefield accepted a cigarette from an American troop. The German lit it up and proceeded to smoke it. The Nazi had many wounds in his chest area. I cringed as I watched the smoke slowly seep out of the holes that I had created in the German's chest.

Chapter 22

I found myself spending many moments thinking about my confrontation with the German on the battlefield. I kept dwelling on the amazing fact that I had actually survived the experience. I knew then like I'd never knew before that someone was looking out for me.

I had faced many near-death experiences, but this one was different. I actually got to look into the eyes of the man that I believed was going to take my life. Under normal circumstances he would have. Then after two amazing incidents of weapon malfunction, the tables suddenly turned and I was the one who controlled whether the German would live or die.

I thought a lot about the German that I had faced off with. I couldn't help but picture the horrible sight of the German as he smoked the cigarette that was given to him and the smoke that rolled out of the wounds in his chest. I wondered whether he had survived or not. I even continue to wonder about that to this day. I never found out if the German lived or died.

I then also found myself thinking about the implications of this to me personally. It's a little bit like the near death situations that many of us find ourselves faced with each day. It seems that after facing death whether it is on a battlefield in Germany, or narrowly missing being hit by an oncoming automobile we are changed. We are changed in what can be considered a good way. We are so thankful to be alive that we hopefully start appreciating life itself. These near death experiences sometimes cause us to take a closer look at our life and how we're spending it. Are we spending time on the things in life that are really important, or have we let the so-called "rat race" choke out our zeal for life? I found myself contemplating these weighty issues as our unit continued to push even further inside the German border.

The next few weeks continued to consist of brutal battle after battle. The Germans continued to fight fiercely as we made our way inside the German border. Our unit fought in battles throughout Germany. We fought in Cologne, which looked very familiar to me since it was the sight of the prisoner of war camp and my dash to the German-Belgium border. We also fought in the German cities of Dusseldorf, where I was hit in the leg by shrapnel for which I received my Purple Heart, Eisen, and Frankfurt along with many other small towns and villages along the way.

As the month of April began it became more and more apparent that it was no longer a matter of if we would win the war in Europe, but when we would win it. The once powerful Nazi regime was in shambles.

The Allied brain trusts were already planning their post-war strategy. This posed more possible problems that in most war time alliances because of the precarious relationship between the United States and the Soviets. The two forms of government were so vastly different ideologically that it made it almost impossible to come to terms of agreement in almost any matter of significance. Really the only reason that the dubious alliance was formed was because of both sides intense dislike for one Adolph Hitler. Had this one common enemy not risen at this time, there is no way that the pact would have been sealed.

The relations were already very strained after several incidents causing a certain amount of mistrust among the parties. Whereas it seemed as if Allied victory in Europe was imminent, if there was a split of the two major Allies things could change drastically.

Looking back at wartime strategy this was really Hitler's best chance at turning things around and changing the tide of battle into the Nazi's favor. Word had it that Hitler realized this very fact, but was unable to come up with effective strategy to facilitate the split.

Hitler seemed to get a little momentum and boost from the sad news that we received on April 12, 1945. On that day we got word that the President of the United States, Franklin Delano Roosevelt had passed away. It was devastating news to an army on the battlefield to hear that their country's leader had fallen, no matter a troop's political preference.

F.D.R., the thirty-second president of the United States served in office from 1933 to 1945 following the very unpopular Hoover administration. He was, just a few months before his death, elected to an unprecedented fourth term in office. His lengthy tenure as president served to provoke the passing of the twenty-second amendment to the constitution shortly after Roosevelt's death. The amendment limited a president to two elected terms of service.

Franklin Roosevelt had served as President of the United States during arguably the two greatest crisis in United States history up to that point – the great depression of the 1930's and of course World War II. His leadership was critical in bringing the United States through these most trying events.

He had greatly expanded the role of the federal government in our society. His extensive domestic programs dubbed as the New Deal included many far-reaching reforms within the free enterprise system. His creations included the Work Projects Administration (W.P.A.), the Tennessee Valley Authority (T.V.A.), and of course the Social Security Act.

Only a little more than a month earlier, Roosevelt had returned from the Yalta Conference of 1945. There he had made several agreements with the Russians. Those agreements included the nature of a post-war international organization, which would lead to the development of the United Nations. He also had reached a pact laying out the military occupation and free elections in Europe. They also had reached agreement on the division of Germany following Allied victory over Adolf Hitler and his Third Reich regime.

Roosevelt suffered through poor health throughout his adult life. He was diagnosed with Polio in 1921 and had a much-reported battle with the debilitating disease during his tenure as President. During his later years he was relegated to a wheelchair much of the time.

He died of a massive cerebral hemorrhage while on a respite in Warm Springs, Georgia. He died knowing that the bulk of his plans for victory had come to pass. He also knew of the very significant problems that were developing with the Soviet Union. Before he died the Russians had already begun to show signs of the disdain they would show for the agreements they had made with Roosevelt at the Yalta Conference. Stalin had already broken their commitment for free elections in the occupied countries of Eastern Europe.

Shortly after Roosevelt's death, his vice-president, Harry S. Truman was sworn in as the thirty-third President of the United States. He would take office at a most crucial crossroads in world history. In only a few short months he would make some decisions that would change the course of the war.

It really seemed odd that Roosevelt was no longer around. He had been President of the United States for more than twelve years. He had taken office when I was only seven years old. He was the only president that I really could remember. It really took some time to get used to thinking of Harry S. Truman as our president. He would quickly have to prove himself.

As victory in Germany became ever more eminent, many new issues were being debated among the officials of both the United States and the Soviet Union. It seemed that the thing that had brought the two together, the common enemy, Adolph Hitler and Nazi Germany was becoming less and less of a rallying point. Tensions were high as the Russians and our leaders were debating the issues of the mapping out of the post-war world order.

Our forces were closing in on Berlin from the West while the Soviets were moving closer and closer to the German capital with each passing day. There were many schools of thought as to how we should proceed with our strategy. Some leaders wanted us to get to Berlin as fast as possible, seeing it as the crown jewel in the European spoils. Pursuing this course of action would in effect make it a race against the Soviets to get to Berlin first and secure the capital city. Others thought that the risks of going into Berlin far outweighed the advantages gained by being the first army in Berlin. The debate continued as we pushed through Germany.

Taking Berlin would have had its positive points. There was the fact that the first army in there would get the opportunity to take the lead in bringing in Nazi leaders for possible trial in world court for crimes of war that had been widely reported. It would have given us a chance to secure Nazi documents of interest that would tell the tale of the goings on in the upper most parts of the Nazi regime. Maybe most importantly the first army in Berlin would have the upper hand in setting up the capital for the implementing of the post-war government of Germany.

Many of our wartime braintrusts believed that it was extremely crucial that we be the first army to reach Berlin. Many of these leaders did not trust Stalin and the Soviets. They had already shown signs of reason for that mistrust by their reluctance for going through with the free elections that Stalin had agreed to at Yalta. Many of our leaders believed that war with the Soviets was eminent and it would be much easier to take Berlin now than have to go in at a later time and try to dislodge the Soviets from the German capital a short time later.

General Eisenhower was of the belief that while taking Berlin would most assuredly have its advantages that those advantages were not worth the possible costs that the operation would bring. He felt that the final onslaught involved in the taking of Berlin would result in very heavy casualties.

The General stayed true to his military strategy in his beliefs. He thought that the taking of Berlin was merely a political maneuver and did not make good military tactical sense. Eisenhower believed that we should pursue the enemy leaders and their armies, as he believed they would try to take refuge in the area of the Alps, as they realized the impending fall of Berlin. He believed it crucial to get to the Alps before these remnants of the German Army made it to the mountains where he feared they could carry out a fanatical resistance. Eisenhower felt it to be better strategy to crush these small pockets of Nazi armies once and for all while letting the Russian Army incur the very heavy casualties that most assuredly would result from the taking of the German capital of Berlin.

Eisenhower convinced the other leaders that his strategy was the way to go, so we headed for the mountains and an impending date with the Nazi Army that was retreating from Berlin and into the Alps. The strategy that Eisenhower played out has been much debated over the years, but one thing is very clear. He was definitely right about the fact that the taking of Berlin would be very costly. With our armies moving to squelch the remaining resistance in the mountains, the Soviets marched toward Berlin. The taking of Berlin would eventually cost the Russians the lives of approximately 100,000 of their troops.

Even with his capital crumbling around him Adolph Hitler refused to surrender. He had been unsuccessful in his last ditch effort to divide the Allied forces and defeat was eminent. His once mighty and powerful Third Reich was now reduced to rubble. His dream of world dominance had failed miserably.

Hitler had received word that on April 28 his long time ally, Italian Dictator, Benito Mussolini had been shot along with his mistress and his body hanged publicly. Two days later on April 30, 1945, fearing that a similar humiliating fate awaited him, Adolph Hitler committed suicide in his bunker in Berlin. He took his life, as did Eva Braun, who Hitler had married the day before.

The end had come for the German political and government leader who had risen to become one of the twentieth century's most powerful dictators. He had converted Germany into a fully militarized society and in search of world domination had launched World War II in 1939. Hitler, who had built his Nazi party using anti-Semitism as the keystone of its propaganda and policies, caused the horrific slaughter of Jews and many others who he considered inferior.

The brutal dictator relied on his secret police, the Gestapo to intimidate his opponents, while amazingly enough many Germans enthusiastically supported him. His massive armament drive had almost totally wiped out unemployment in Germany. His many apparent successes in foreign policy had impressed the nation and helped to build support for his regime inside Germany.

He had particularly appealed to the many who believed that Germany had been humiliated by World War I and the Treaty of Versailles of 1919. Many world leaders believed that the treaty that effectively ended World War I was much too harsh on the Germans. Many Germans still felt the bitterness of the effects of the treaty many years later.

Adolph Hitler possessed a very forceful charismatic personality and knew how to appeal to people's baser instincts. He was a master at using people's fears and insecurities to promote his agenda.

Adolph Hitler's death brought down his Third Reich's rule in Germany. The German dictator's impact was wholly destructive and nothing of what he spent the years of his rule building survived after he was gone from the scene. It's still very frightening to this day to think that a man of his intense hatred could rise to such enormous power in our world.

We continued to take part in the implementation of Eisenhower's plan of attack in the finishing off of the Germans. Our unit made its way toward the Alps. We were set up on Harz Mountain in the German Alps. It was located in central Germany between the Elbe and the Weser Rivers.

Our instructions were to hold the mountain while preventing any remnants of the German army from taking up refuge in the mountainous region. If they did manage to make it into the mountainous region, it would be next to impossible to flush them out without costing us many lives.

Our unit managed to secure the mountain very swiftly without running into much of any fighting. We had evidently made it to the area ahead of any escaping German pockets of resistance. With our units already in position on the mountain, it would have been literally suicidal for the Nazis that were on the run from Berlin to try to make it into the mountains.

After we had pretty much settled in on Harz Mountain we just waited for our next instructions. Some of the guys thought we were crazy to let the Russians have Berlin, but most of them were glad not to have to go down there and fight what would be a battle with heavy casualties.

While the Russians fought for control of Berlin, we just sat tight and waited on the mountain. We would sit up there and listen to the battle that was raging in the capital. It sounded as if the fighting was fierce as the Soviets finished off the remaining resistance in Berlin.

I guess I didn't really think too much about the significance of the battle for Berlin. I really didn't worry too much at that time about whether we were making the right tactical move by letting the Russians take Berlin. I was just glad that I didn't have to be down there in another battle.

Chapter 23

The Harz Mountains were located in the central part of Germany just outside of Berlin. It was an absolutely beautiful area of the world. I was awfully sorry that I had to visit these mountains under these circumstances, but they were beautiful none the less. I knew that I also would like to visit this area under somewhat more pleasant circumstances some time.

The mountains were situated between the Elbe and Weser Rivers in a very secluded and seemingly peaceful area. Several miles east of us there was absolutely anything but peace.

Because of the elevation and the distance from Berlin we had been able to watch the Russian Army march on Berlin. They rolled in the German capital in masses. It felt a little funny just sitting by while the Russians went in, but who was I to question a military genius like Eisenhower? As I mentioned earlier I really didn't relish the idea of fighting another battle anyway. It was fine with me just to sit back and let the Russians do the dirty work.

Of the thousands of Soviets that we saw move in on Berlin many never walked out. The Soviets defeat of the small pocket of resistance left was eminent, but it would be very costly. The Russians went in and for an extended time period we could hear the battle raging on down below.

After we established ourselves on the mountain and secured it, we pretty much just took it easy and listened to the battle between the Nazi resistance and the large Soviet contingent. It was the first time in many weeks that we had felt so relaxed.

Day after day the battle continued. Even though the Nazis were on their last leg, they didn't give up easily. Many fought to the death defending the capital. Even with their long time leader gone, they fought on.

Waiting there on Harz Mountain did have its good points. As I mentioned we got a chance to relax and rest a little for the first time in weeks. It was also very beautiful scenery, but there were also some problems, some very real problems.

As had happened to our unit many times in our trek across Europe, we had outrun our supplies. This time our supplies were basically non-existent. It appeared to make little difference with our shortage of ammunition, because if things continued to go the direction that it seemed, we would not have to expend much ammunition in securing the mountain.

Some of the shortages made it very inconvenient, but the biggest shortage was our low food supply. Actually it was only low for a small length of time, then it was not low any more – it was gone. That's right we were out of food. We began to root harder for the Soviets to finish off the Nazis because we knew that there would be no more shipments of supplies until the battle for Berlin was finished. It became very questionable as to whether we could hold on or not.

Faced with the thought of no food for maybe many days, we were forced to improvise. Fortunately for us Harz Mountain was a wooded wilderness type area. This opened the area to various forms of wildlife. The members of our unit then turned from hunting the enemy to hunting wild game.

In our stay on the mountain we had viewed many types of wild animals running around in the area. We were not too picky as to the type of animal that would constitute our much-needed meal. The meal of choice though was one that was made up of wild deer.

We had seen many deer in the area. Since we really didn't have to focus on the enemy, we could turn our almost complete attention to hunting down the deer for a meal of venison.

Many of the men were avid hunters, so not only were they hunting for the animals to provide food for the men of the unit, but they were also able to participate in a sport that they used as recreation back home. It was the first time in I don't know how long that we actually were able to participate in an activity that was somewhat enjoyable. It was fun hunting there in the mountains of Germany, but in our case there was a little more pressure to actually bag something when we realized that whether or not we would be able to have something that resembled a decent meal depended on our hunt being a success.

Even though deer can be a very difficult animal to hunt down and kill, we had a pretty decent amount of success. We had become pretty adept at hunting down Nazis, so the deer didn't pose a problem for us in most cases. So, while the Russians continued their assault on Berlin only a few miles away we were busy hunting deer on Harz Mountain. The more that I thought about the strategy that General Eisenhower had implemented, the more I liked it.

The fighting raged on in Berlin for more than two weeks. We continued to survive on the animals that we had rounded up. We got kind of used to the deer meat. When we had a good haul and all of us got plenty to eat, it was actually better food than we were accustomed to before we found ourselves in a severe supply shortage.

As the days continued to pass the shelling and explosions that we were hearing off into the background got a little less severe. The artillery sounds were getting fewer and farther between. We figured that this was probably a very good sign that things might be finally coming to an end. The much less frequent war sounds continued to drag on for several days.

I found myself taking advantage of the time that we had on our hands. I caught up on some much-needed sleep. I also got a chance to kind of collect my thoughts on what I had been through here. I knew that in war that anything could happen, but it looked as if we were not going to have to participate in any more fighting. It appeared that barring any unforeseen skirmishes that I, along with the rest of the surviving members of my unit would in fact make it out of there alive.

I started to think about my survival and how improbable that it had been. I should have been killed several times. The fact that I was apparently going to be allowed to survive was testament to the ever-increasing belief on my part that someone was watching over me.

I also knew that by pursuing Eisenhower's much-debated strategy that the odds of my survival along with the others in my unit were increased infinitely. I shudder to think of what it would have been like to go down into Berlin and try to eliminate the remaining factions of Nazis there.

It was just another case of circumstances intervening and allowing me to escape a fate with death. I wondered many times why I had been allowed to survive while many others were not so fortunate. I remembered Rose talking about the Lord and that His will would be done regardless. The more I looked back on the circumstances and events surrounding my service time, the more I came to believe that my good buddy just may have been right.

I started to believe that for some reason that my fate was to make it out of there alive. I was in no way, shape or form sure as to why I was supposed to make it, but I believed that I was. It gave me a good feeling.

Now don't get me wrong, I wasn't going to test fate. I wasn't going to throw myself in front of a moving jeep, or go running into battle unarmed just daring whomever, or whatever was watching out for me to bring me out of a mess one more time. I figured that with all that I had been through that I had already done more than my share of testing fate.

It did make me feel good, though. It gave me a comforting feeling. Maybe it was given to me to let me be able to cope with the brutal conditions that we had faced in our service. I saw many men who didn't seem to have that same peace. They usually had a difficult time dealing with the horrors of war. Who could blame them? It was absolutely terrible, but for some strange reason I really never had much trouble dealing with it from an emotional standpoint.

Some of the men definitely did have trouble dealing with it. I saw this during our stay on Harz Mountain. Some of the men were just unable to take it easy and relax. I guess they were too keyed up after many months of battlefield conditions. I really felt sorry for them.

Some of these men were very vocal about their battle experiences. They loved to relate the stories of the circumstances they had faced as we were passing the time there on Harz Mountain waiting for the Soviets to do their job.

Many of the men took a very different approach to war stories. They didn't want to talk about their experiences and they didn't want to hear about any of the other men's experiences either. They seemed to just want to forget about what they had been through. It's very hard to blame these men. All of us there had seen and been a part of many incidents in battle that no man should have to face.

We had been witness to brutalities that you could never imagine. We would never have believed it had we not been there to see it with our own eyes. It was difficult to get those horrible pictures out of your head.

I found myself thinking about the different approaches that the men in my unit took to talking about their experiences. I wondered what made some men be able to talk about it very freely while others could not utter a word about the experience. The men seemed to be so different in their attitudes.

I guess I fell somewhere in between the two groups. I didn't exactly love to talk about my experiences like some of the men did. Some of the men seemed to like to brag about their experiences. I didn't go in for that, but I had no hang-ups about conversing with a fellow soldier about the various gruesome events that I had faced. I sometimes felt that it actually helped me get it off my mind to bring it out in the open and talk about it with someone else that had been in similar circumstances and could relate to the way that I felt. This point of view would end up serving me well over the years.

The silence was deafening. The noises of war that we had been hearing for the last couple of weeks were no longer there. We continued to listen very closely for an extended time period – Nothing. The guns were silent. The shelling was silent. The grenades were silent. It was just silent.

Word started to spread all around Harz Mountain that the war in Europe might very well be all over. Our unit still hadn't received any official notification of this, but if the lack of battle sounds were any indication then the war with Nazi Germany had come to an end.

After we waited for a while for the news to be confirmed, we finally got official word in a message delivered to our unit on the two-way radio. The war in Europe was officially over!

Then on that mountain range in Germany, there proceeded to be the most joyous celebration that I had ever been a part of or witnessed in my entire life. The war with Germany was over. It was hard to believe, but it was true. There would be no more battles with the Nazis as the Soviets secured their capital after a lengthy struggle.

The men in our unit were absolutely jubilant. We were all hugging and yes, even kissing each other in celebration of the news that we had long awaited. We were all dancing around in glee at the wonderful news. Men were firing their weapons into the air as we broke the silence that we had been waiting for. Happiness abounded on that mountain. The Russian Army had finally finished the job. They had secured the city of Berlin.

As the Russian Army rolled through the German capital what was left of the Nazis were desperately trying if not to escape, to at least surrender to the U.S. troops and not the Russians. It was widely known how brutally the Germans had treated the Russian people in the lands they had taken from the Soviets temporarily, not to mention the fact that the news was surfacing of Russians being sent to the inhumane concentration camps along with the Jews for extermination.

There was a deep hatred among the Nazis and the Russians. Joseph Stalin, the Soviet leader had basically trusted almost no one. He was widely known for his suspicions in dealing with leaders from other countries regarding foreign policy issues. For some strange reason the Russian leader decided to trust one Adolph Hitler. He signed a non-aggression pact with the Nazi leader, only to have Hitler and the Nazis turn on them and attack the Russians.

For quite some time it appeared that the Germans were headed for Moscow. The German war machine was tuned up and running on all cylinders. If it hadn't been for the entry of the United States into the war in December of 1941 after Pearl Harbor and the extremely brutal weather conditions that the German Army faced in Russia on their way to Moscow, they might well have overrun the Russians.

When the tide turned for the Soviets, it turned quickly and drastically ending now in the Soviets walking the streets of Berlin. The Nazi dictator was dead and the Third Reich was in rubbles.

We heard many stories of the Russians taking out their frustrations on the Nazi prisoners that they were able to bring in. Because of this fact the Germans were desperate to surrender to us and not the Soviets.

The Russians would pay dearly with the loss of many lives for taking the city that had already been partitioned off in negotiations. At that point in time, I, or no one else involved in the process seemed to understand that the division of Berlin would play such a huge part in the relationship between the United States and the Soviet Union over the next few decades as the "cold war" was played out.

The minor suspicions at the end of the war in Europe would turn to bitter differences that would lead to global problems over the next several years. Little did we know at the time that the two countries would seemingly bring the world to the brink of nuclear war on more than one occasion.

That would be in the future, but right now the two countries had just worked together to squash Nazi Germany. It was a precarious union, but one that turned out to be effective none the less.

After German leader, Adolph Hitler's suicide in his bunker in Berlin, the new German leader was Karl Doenitz, who Hitler had pre-appointed to the position before the dictator's death. On May 7, 1945 Doenitz sent General Alfred Jodl to the headquarters of the Supreme Commander of the Allies in Europe, General Dwight D. Eisenhower in Reims. There Jodl, on behalf of Nazi Germany offered his country's unconditional surrender to the Allied forces.

It was now completely official. Adolph Hitler's quest for world domination had come to an end. The war in Europe was now officially over. The next day, May 8, was declared V-E (Victory in Europe) Day.

Chapter 24

Our celebration, as important as it was, was definitely somewhat premature. We knew that it was a victory, but it was only victory in Europe. We knew that we currently had many of our men in the Southwest Pacific trying to finish off the Empire of Japan. What we had heard about the fighting there was mostly positive, but like the battles that I saw in Europe, it supposedly was also very brutal.

While we were doing mop up duty in Europe, the Allied leaders were meeting in what would be their last conference in Potsdam, Germany. The Potsdam Conference was held from July 17 to August 2, 1945. The participants included United States President Harry S. Truman who was making his first appearance at a conference with the other Allied leaders after the death of Franklin Roosevelt. Also there representing Great Britain was Winston Churchill, who was replaced during the conference by Clement Attlee. The third participant was Soviet leader Joseph Stalin.

The three countries confirmed the already agreed to division of Germany. It was settled at Yalta that Germany would be divided into four zones. The leaders established the fact that all Nazis that were suspected of committing war crimes would be held for trial.

The conference brought the first open major disagreements between the Soviets and the other two leaders. The United States and Great Britain refused to accept the pro-Soviet provisional government set up in Poland. They contended that the government was not democratic as was previously agreed to.

The United States and Great Britain also wanted to set up democratic governments in the other countries of Eastern Europe that the Soviets had liberated from the Nazis. Truman and Attlee wanted free elections held in Romania, Bulgaria, and Hungary. Stalin wanted the recognition of the puppet regimes that the Soviets had set up in these countries.

This was definitely a sign of things to come. It was one of the first of many differences between the Allies. The dubious alliance was hanging by a thread and would prove to not last much longer than did Hitler, the common enemy that united the nations together.

There were rumors circulating that we had developed a "super weapon" to use on the Japanese. Later we would learn this to be true.

On August 6, 1945 we used the first nuclear weapon in history. On that day the United States of America dropped an atomic bomb on the Japanese city of Hiroshima.

The effects were absolutely devastating. The city was demolished. It was unlike anything used before in the history of man. It created a combination of fire and extreme radiation that left the Japanese city in rubbles and a nation of people wondering what had hit them.

Giving the Japanese a couple of days to consider surrender, the United States waited until August 9, 1945 to drop the second atomic weapon used in battle on the Japanese city of Nagasaki. The massive destruction in Hiroshima was duplicated in the second city that felt the effects of the dawning of the nuclear age.

After being hit by the two massive strikes, the Japanese decided to seek terms of surrender. After some negotiations with the Allies, the Japanese signed a document of surrender on the United States battleship, Missouri in Tokyo Bay.

The real celebration could now finally begin, as the Japanese surrender was official. September 2 was dubbed as V-J (Victory in Japan) Day. The victory was now fully complete!

While all this was taking place, I was going through the process of being released from the army. After victory was ours, the army began the lengthy process of commissioning men out of the army. This was done using a point system to decide in what order we would be able to be sent back stateside. The points that we received were based on service time, injuries suffered, and points were also given for time as a prisoner of war.

With this criteria being used, I had accumulated many points. I had been in service in Europe for more than a year. I had received three separate wounds, for one of which I was presented a Purple Heart by General Eisenhower at his headquarters in Paris, France. It was one of the greatest honors of my life. I had also spent time in a German prisoner of war camp which I was awarded points for.

Because of these factors, I was one of the first to get to be sent home. I was absolutely thrilled. The process took a while, but I was eventually on my way. I was first shipped to Le Harve, France by truck. It was not too long before I boarded an Italian ship for the long trip back home to the United States.

I spent twenty days on that ship. It seemed even longer as I was anticipating setting foot back home in the U.S. After the long ocean voyage we eventually arrived in Norfolk, Virginia. It sure felt good to be back in the Good Ole' U.S.A.

I had wondered many times over the last several months whether or not this day would ever come. It was difficult to believe that I was actually back in the United States after all I had been through. I was back in the country that I had spent time in Europe fighting for. I couldn't help but think about all the men that would never get the chance to step foot back in the country that they loved so much. They would never get the opportunity to get a taste of the freedom that these men had bravely given their lives to help preserve. It caused me to reflect a lot about what I had been through in my service to my beloved country.

I wasn't sure what I should do first. It had been so long since I had been in this position that it was hard to adjust to. After we were unloaded from the massive Italian ocean liner, military officials warmly greeted us. We were congratulated for our service to the United States. All of us were then taken for a much deserved and long over due meal.

We were given steak with all the trimmings. It was absolutely delicious. I almost had forgotten what steak tasted like. I think I ate like I never had before. It was great. I still remember watching those men as they stuffed themselves after doing without food of that quality for so long. I did exactly the same thing. After I finished the luscious meal, I was absolutely stuffed.

I remember talking with the other men as we dined. All of us seemed to have a particular hankering for some specific kind of food. Before we began our big meal many of the men would describe how they looked forward to a juicy steak.

I had a hankering for something special also. I know it sounds odd, but the one thing that I was really craving was a nice tall, cold, glass of milk. I know it probably wasn't the most popular item with all the entrees that many of the men were anticipating, but it was what I wanted. When we were finally served, I drank glass after glass of milk. It had never tasted so good.

After a short two or three hour stay in Virginia, I boarded a train to begin my trip home. We headed west and eventually to my home in Southern Illinois. We passed through many places on our voyage. Many of the men got off the train at locations all across the country. I got the chance to see many happy reunions as we made our way closer and closer to Illinois.

I enjoyed watching the people involved in the reunions. I liked to watch the faces of the men as they first saw their hometown. I would always see a broad smile appear on their faces. I especially liked to watch the men as they first saw members of their family members who were waiting for them.

More often than not it was a very emotional scene. I would witness the eyes of those men light up like Christmas trees when they first caught the eye of their family, which sometimes included moms and dads. I saw many a mom crying her eyes out at the sight of her son unloading from that train. I'm sure it was a sight that many mothers thought might never come. Most times the mother was not alone in shedding a few tears at this moment. The fathers and usually even the returning service men joined in the shedding of tears.

Sometimes it was a sweetheart there waiting for her beau to return. It could be a young lady who wondered if her plans of marriage and a life with the man she loved would ever get the chance to come to fruition. The sight of their man getting off that train confirmed that their dreams might well comes true.

Many times it would be a wife who had been longing for many months to see the sight of her beloved husband returning home from battle. Sometimes that wife had children with her to help greet daddy. Sometimes it was the first time that daddy had laid eyes on their child that had only been a hopeful expectation when he left home. It was truly a very emotional scene.

Seeing these touching family reunions made me think of the people who were waiting for someone that would never come. As the many happy welcome homes were going on, I knew that there were also many instances of overwhelming grief at the loss of a father, son, brother, uncle, or friend.

There were many incredibly sad situations like these in our country, but there were even more of them around the world. I knew that some of the other countries involved in the war had experienced even more casualties than we did. Then I would ponder my personal impact on this. I thought about my experiences in battle and estimated that I probably was involved in the capture of about 15 enemy troops. I wondered if they ever made it home to their families. I also estimated that I was myself personally responsible for killing approximately twenty enemy men. I knew that these men would never return to a waiting grieving family back home.

I would sometimes dwell on the killings. I remembered how very rough it was to have to be a part of them at first. I used to think about how I didn't even know that man as a person. I would wonder if he had been a lot like me. He may have been a very good man, a very nice human being with a family back home. As a soldier we were trained to keep these thoughts out of our heads. We were trained to take the attitude that a good soldier had to kill or be killed. As true as this saying was, this was still the most difficult part of war for me.

The family gatherings also made me think about my own family back in Southern Illinois. I wondered about them a lot. I wondered how they were and what they were doing. I was very curious as to whether or not my parents and siblings missed me. I thought a lot about my childhood and my relationship with my family. I knew that we had not always had the best of family harmony. I hoped that even though we had our share of problems that they would put those things aside and be glad to see me make it back to them alive. It would not be long now before I would get the chance to find out one way or another.

I eventually arrived in Camp Grant, Illinois. I was mastered out of the army on December 13, 1945. I then boarded what we used to call a slow train and headed to Johnston City, Illinois, a small city just a few miles from my home.

During the trip south on the train, my leg started giving me some trouble. Shrapnel had hit me in the leg and the metal was still in there. I couldn't put my full weight on it and it continued to ache constantly like there was a thorn or something like that in my leg. It gave me trouble through the entire ride south.

As we got closer and closer to Johnston City, I was anxious with anticipation at making it home after these many months away. Even though we had our differences, I was sure looking forward to seeing everybody. I could just see the incredible sight in my mind. I could see my mom and stepfather there waiting for me. I pictured my mom crying at the happy sight of my return. I pictured my stepfather shaking my hand and congratulating me on my honorable service to my country. I could see the proud look on his face after speaking of my military duty.

I could also picture in my mind the sight of my siblings lining up to take their turn at greeting me after my long trip away from home. I pictured us taking some time and catching up with each other after my voyage away from home. Yeah, I could just picture this in my mind. Unfortunately that would be the one and only place that I would see this sight.

We arrived in Johnston City after a very long ride, where I got off the train. Like most of the other places we had stopped before, there were some very touching reunions. I found myself watching these moments while I wondered whether I would get the same chance to reunite with my family.

I got off of the train in Johnston City in anticipation of a warm greeting from my family. I looked around the area and found no one. There was no one there. I was devastated, though not surprised. I tried not to let this disappointment get me down, but it was difficult.

I then noticed a gentleman wandering around the area. He appeared to be looking for someone. He approached me and asked me if my name was Cecil Rains. I told him that it was. He told me that his name was Bunton Crow. He was a local recruiter for Woodman of the World and he had volunteered to escort me to my parent's new home. While I was in service my parents had moved from Pittsburg to Johnston City. I didn't know him at the time, but I came to know him after this meeting. He showed me the way to my family's new home.

I made it to the door. I waited for a moment as I prepared for the anticipated warm welcome I would receive from my family. I opened the door and saw my parents for the fist time in several months. They looked surprised for a moment and then they approached me.

They greeted me and very commonly shook my hand. No hugs. No kisses. No emotion. It was nothing like the very heartwarming reunions I had witnessed on the trip home. My parents greeted me as if I just returned home from a short trip to the store to get a loaf of bread.

Did they not know where I had spent the last several months? If they only knew how many times over that time period that I had come so dangerously close to never making it back. I had just returned home after risking my life in a world war and my parents had absolutely no reaction to speak of.

To say that I was let down was a major understatement. I had come home expecting a hero's welcome and my parents barely made notice of my entrance into the home after not seeing me for several months. I was so anxious to share my experiences that I had been through with my family and they really didn't seem the least bit interested in what I had to say.

I had been a part of the largest land invasion in history at Normandy during D-Day. I had taken part in the largest land battle in World War II during the Battle of the Bulge. I took part in these and many other very crucial battles.

Didn't they know that they were in the presence of a decorated soldier? I had received the Purple Heart, Silver Star, two Oak Leaf Clusters, and also a Prisoner of War Medal among others.

The funny thing about this was that I really didn't care about those things, at least at that moment. I just wanted them to care about me. I just wanted them to be glad to see me even if I returned without a single honor. To this day, I still cannot fathom their reaction, or I should say their lack of one.

I used the next several months to try to relax and try to let my shrapnel wounds heal properly. After a while my wounds healed pretty well and I really wasn't limited by any of my injuries I had suffered in battle. I also used the time to acclimate myself to what I wanted to do with the rest of my life.

During that time I came to grips with the fact that as much as I would have liked my family to be more loving and caring toward me, that in all likelihood this would never happen. I finally realized that I could only control my own attitude and myself. I couldn't make others feel something that wasn't there, or make them express something that they were not comfortable expressing. The sooner I realized that, then the sooner that I could go on with my life. That's exactly what I did. I had to get on with my life on my own.

I stayed about a year in Johnston City. I then decided it was time to move on and get out on my own. I bought a one-way bus ticket to Chicago. I got a job as a truck driver with Brody Trucking Company. I would later work as their warehouse foreman. I also did some minor work for the FBI on the side.

Although I seemed to deal with the traumas of war much better than many of the men I had encountered, my service did have an enormous effect on the rest of my life. There was a period of time after the end of the war that I found myself becoming very nervous and tense in dealing with everyday life. I would go to sleep and dream of the many killings and the massive destruction that I had been witness to during my time spent in World War II. To this day, I still on very rare occasions have flashbacks, reliving some of the more traumatic experiences that I lived through during my time of service in the army. As terrible of an experience as this can be, I never let this engulf me. I never let it dominate my thoughts or feelings. It never changed my attitude that I was proud to be a part of World War II and honored to fight for my country.

While living in Northern Illinois I met Helen Foss from Aurora, and married her on June 28, 1951. We raised a large family together. I was determined to create in my own family the type of loving and caring relationship that was lacking in my family as I was growing up.

After several years of trying to wrestle with some of the things that my buddy, Rose had spoken of concerning God and Jesus Christ, I finally gave my life to the Lord. I accepted Jesus Christ as my personal Savior and was baptized with my son, Danny in 1964.

Even though I was slow to give my life to the Lord, I had always had those same feelings that I had in the Army that God was watching out for me. I knew that the only way that I could have come through the many trials and tribulations of both my childhood years and my years that I spent in service in World War II was that the Lord was watching out for me.

Helen and I were married for thirty-eight wonderful years before she passed away on September 17, 1989. After her passing I spent a long time grieving. I still miss her terribly. Our children served as a great comfort during this difficult time. My grandson, Sean served as a great help in filling the void left by Helen's death. I thank God for my wonderful family.

Chapter 25

I have truly been blessed throughout my life. I have had to live through my share of suffering over the years, but I have always been able to look at things from a positive point of view.

My parents were very strict on me when I was growing up. That being said, I still believe that this type of upbringing had some positive effects on me.

Even though I didn't practice the sort of discipline with my kids that my parents did with me, I did come away from the experience learning many things. They instilled in me to respect not only them as my parents, but also others that I came in contact with. This characteristic is sometimes lacking in youngsters today. Now don't get me wrong, I don't endorse the rough treatment I received as a child to instill respect to our children. I'm just saying that all I could do was try to make something good out of something bad and I did learn respect for others.

Also living through that tough childhood I found myself able to be compassionate to others. I knew very well what it was like to not be given the compassion and caring that a child desperately needs. This fact let me very much sympathize with others who I felt were hurting. I knew what hurt was and how devastating it can be, this allowed me to better put myself in other people's situations that they were facing. It was another instance of my taking something negative and turning it into a positive situation.

Most people would also consider having to live through and take part in World War II to be a negative experience, as it very much was. The war in which countries housing three-fourths of the earth took part and around 110 million served in some form of military service was absolutely devastating to our planet. Before the final surrender of Japan brought it to an end, there were approximately 60 million people killed by its effects.

If I had been given a choice in the matter, I would have preferred that the war never happened at all. Unfortunately I wasn't given that choice. Since we were faced with the ominous attack on Pearl Harbor and our country would be forced to fight for the freedom that we had become accustomed to, I felt it my duty to volunteer to take part in the defense of my country. I would not wish what happened to me in my service to happen to anyone. I did, however, take away many insights from my service that helped me in dealing with later life.

I came away from those fields in which I was surrounded by death with a much greater respect for human life. I realized how precious life is and how if we're not careful we can waste ours. I remember the times that I faced death. We faced death twenty-four hours a day seven days a week. I personally had come face to face with death in several circumstances that appeared that there would be no way to survive. I did survive and it taught me a lot.

I remember thinking in those situations of all the things I would like to do. I remember thinking that if I'm just allowed to survive this then I'm never going to take life for granted again. I believe that many people get caught up in everyday life so much that they forget the really important things in life. When you are forced to face death on a daily basis, it helps you remember the important things in life. My service has had a profound affect on my attitude toward every day life. I now realize how precious life really is.

Another aspect of war that served to teach me the value of human life was watching the actions of other men on the battlefield, heroic actions. The sacrifices that men made to preserve the freedom that we have in our country were absolutely too numerous to mention. The heroic action of my best friend, Rose had a very profound effect on the rest of my life.

I had never really experienced friendship until I met Rose. He was my first real close buddy. I knew that friends cared for one another, I just didn't know how deep this caring could actually be. Rose taught me how deep that his care for me was when he sacrificed his life to save mine. During my life since my service in World War II I have had many friends. Fortunately none of them have been faced with circumstances that forced them to sacrifice their life for mine just as I have never given my life for a friend. Because of Rose, though, I now understand that if faced with a situation in which I needed to give my life to save someone, I would do it without even thinking twice. I have always appreciated the friends that have come into my life and the love and caring that I feel from them. Even had I survived in some other manner on that battlefield, I would never have had the many friends that I have been blessed with let alone appreciating them appropriately if it were not for the actions of my friend that showed me what friendship really is.

My friend Rose not only saved my life once on the day in battle, he really saved my life twice. At that moment in my life, I had never entered into a personal relationship with Christ. If I had died that day, I would have faced eternity without the Lord.

So you see, in reality Rose saved me twice. He saved my life physically, of course by throwing his body on that grenade in battle. More importantly he saved my spiritual life, by giving me another opportunity to be saved by Christ. I am convinced that the Lord sent him into my life for that specific purpose. He had set up the moment by witnessing to me and praying for me on a daily basis. He then preserved for me the opportunity to ask Christ into my heart.

For many years it used to bother me that Rose had given his life for mine. I felt guilty that I had lived and he had died. I felt almost responsible for his death. After accepting Christ as my Savior and now understanding what this means, I realize that Rose is in Heaven with the Lord and he is better off than we are here on earth. It helped me deal with the loss of my friend.

After the experience of meeting and marrying my wife, Helen and the life that we were able to spend together, and now with my children and grandchildren, I knew that the Lord had spared my life for a reason. He had let me see a positive family experience. He allowed me to be a part of a loving and caring family in my adult years. I will always be grateful for that opportunity that I never would have gotten had he not preserved my life though my childhood and the war.

Many of the veterans that I had come into contact with over the years had been reluctant to talk about their war service. I'm sure that these men had never come to grips with the brutality of war. They most likely had not dealt with the horrible things that they saw and were forced to participate in.

In many cases men came home fresh from these traumatic experiences and did not want to talk about them. They didn't want to feel as if they were reliving the horrors by talking about them. I'm sure there were many instances in which men never mentioned their experiences again. It has been well proven that in many cases this way of dealing with trauma is not mentally healthy. Whereas I didn't relish reliving these experiences, for some reason I was always able to understand that it was healthy to talk about them and not keep them inside and let these feelings begin to eat you up inside. I have to admit that I was one of the fortunate ones in this respect. Many men just never could deal with it.

I still at this stage in my life felt that the Lord had something in store for me. I believed that he had something more that he specifically wanted me to do with the rest of my life. I would soon understand just what that purpose was.

I soon had an opportunity open up that made it clear what I could do with my life that would have a positive impact on the lives of others. Over the last several years I had not done a lot of talking about my experiences in World War II. Only occasionally I would discuss some of the aspects of my service with someone when they would hear that I was a World War II veteran.

Word evidently got around a little and I was asked to speak about my experiences to a class of kids. I was a little nervous and also skeptical at first. I wondered if youths today would be interested in hearing about my exploits so many years earlier. I pondered whether or not telling my story could make a difference. I soon got my answer.

I was a hit, if I do say so myself. The kids seemed not only to enjoy the stories, but also have a deep interest in hearing about the war and the time period that it represented. I was overwhelmed by the reaction. Soon schools all around Southern Illinois were asking me to speak to their classes.

I really had the mistaken idea that these kids were told about World War II and the time period by parents or in most cases maybe grandparents, or even great grandparents. I found that this was not true. Sometimes the child's grandparents had passed away, or maybe they had been reluctant to talk about their experiences of war.

Most of the kids seemed to only know about World War II from what they had gotten out of textbooks. I have nothing against textbooks. They can be used very effectively to aid drastically in the learning process, but there is no way that books can as accurately depict history as can one who lived through it.

I quickly came to the realization that many kids had a burning desire to hear first hand about the past and that they were not getting this in most cases, for whatever reason from other older family members. I then knew what the Lord had given me to do with the rest of my life. I have dedicated myself to spending the rest of my life speaking to as many kids in as many classrooms as I possibly can.

After spending several years at this mission of speaking to youngsters, I recently was slowed by some health problems. I had to have major heart bypass surgery. Once again the Lord was definitely watching over me. He brought me through this minor roadblock and once again I am planning to speak to classes after having to take some time off for my recovery.

At the time of this writing, I currently live in Mt. Vernon, a town in Southern Illinois near my boyhood home. I have remarried. My wife, Loretta and I are members of the Bonnie Church of God and worship together on a regular basis. I enjoy spending time with my family and friends that I have been so blessed with.

I have truly been blessed in this life in too many ways for me to mention. I have had to suffer as has most everyone, but I have, with the Lords help, managed to keep a positive attitude. I believe that this attitude is vital in finding true happiness. I also hear about the "Good Ole' Days". I believe that sometimes as in my case of my childhood, that the "Good Ole' Days" were not really so good. I believe that the present is actually the best time because the present is the only time that we have the privilege of being able to live in right now. I enjoy, as do most people that reach my age, talking about the past, but I also realize that I can only live in the present and I thank God for the opportunity to live that present the best way I possibly can.

I hope to use this time to deliver my message to children throughout Southern Illinois. I want to let them know that no matter what circumstances you face in life that you can deal with it. You can rise above difficult family situations. I want to inspire children who face these difficult conditions. I want them to know that I am living proof that this can happen. I had to go through a tough childhood, but I managed to rise above this with a positive outlook and most importantly the Lord Jesus Christ.

There's an old saying that states that if we are ignorant of our past, then we are destined to repeat it. If I have anything to say about it, our younger generation will not be ignorant concerning World War II. I do this with the hope that these young people will not have to go through the same thing.

I have many kids ask me if I would do the same thing if I had to do it all again. I have no trouble answering that question. I would most certainly do it all over again. If our country were faced with the same circumstances, I would not hesitate to do it again. As I look into the eyes of those youngsters in those classrooms and realize the freedom that they have because of the sacrifice that many made in World War II, I have no doubts that we did the right thing and that we would do it all again.

As I'm sure you can easily see, my life has been no "piece of cake", but my life has always been in the hands of the Lord. My motto is these five words: "My Life Belongs To God."

This has been my story. Many other stories are out there, many stories of men and their sacrifices. In some ways maybe my story is unusual, but in many more ways it's probably very common. Though every story played out in the unfolding of the events surrounding World War II is different in various ways, each of these accounts deserves to be told. It's a fitting tribute to the members of what has been dubbed "The Greatest Generation". I don't consider myself great, I just am honored to have been able to be amongst the men that served our country. I hope that the telling of my story will inspire others to do the same.

I have been truly blessed throughout my lifetime. I owe it all to Christ. For me to have come through what I have to get to this point, I definitely know that the Lord has been watching over Rains.

Conclusion

Cecil Rains passed away October 15, 2002. We had only weeks earlier signed the contract with JoNa Books to publish *Watching Over Rains*. While I regret that Cecil didn't actually get to live to see the book go to print, I am truly thankful that he got to sign the contract and knew that his story would be told. In fact, he spent the last moments of his life passing out preorder forms for *Watching Over Rains*.

It is difficult for me to convey how fortunate I feel to be the one that actually put Cecil's story down on paper. As I think about the writing of *Watching Over Rains* I think very little about the actual sitting in front of the computer putting down copy and very much about talking with Cecil about his experiences. The number of living World War II veterans is diminishing and while many of the stories are not as eventful as Cecil's, they all deserve to be told. Our country would be much the better for it.

We have also had interest in our screenplay version of *Watching Over Rains*. It is a story that would play out wonderfully on the screen. Cecil always enjoyed discussing the potential movie and who would play him. I am told that he had written down Tom Hanks' address for future reference. It never hurts to be prepared.

Though he liked telling his stories, he was not boastful at all. I remember once as I was ready to begin writing I asked Cecil if there was anything he had left out. He then thought of the incident of being bitten by a rattlesnake in basic training and almost dying. That was not an experience that many would forget. Cecil's life was filled with these types of incidents.

Cecil enjoyed telling his story at schools and other organizations. I always enjoyed watching Cecil talk to my classes. He had such a great rapport with the kids, and adults as well. Cecil had a way of meeting someone for the first time and making him or her feel as if they had known him their whole life.

On the one-year anniversary of the tragic events of September 11, 2001, Cecil, in failing health spoke at Mt. Vernon Countryside Manor where my wife, Marla is the Administrator. It was the last of his many public appearances where he touched many lives relating his World

War II experiences. There is no way to measure the impact he has had on the lives of people throughout Southern Illinois.

Though we tried to relate the major events in Cecil's life, there are no doubt just as many more that are not written down that should be. I have heard many stories in which Cecil helped someone in one way or another. Some of these were of the spectacular type that occurred on the battlefield in life and death situations. Likely more often these acts occurred in every day life with his family and friends.

Cecil's life could serve as a great lesson to many. He had a difficult life in many ways, but he didn't dwell on that. In fact, he tried to look for ways he could learn from his past and help others. With the Lord's guidance, Cecil made the most of his life. Instead of dwelling on the negative events of his childhood, he chose to be a positive person. He always thanked God for his many blessings, most importantly his family and friends.

Cecil Rains was not only a great soldier, but more importantly he was a great man of God. He will truly be missed.

T.J. Howard

Bibliography

1. Encyclopedia Britannica – Britannica.com

2. 1998 Grolier Multimedia Encyclopedia – 1997 Grolier Interactive Inc.

3. Microsoft Encarta 98 Encyclopedia – 1993-1997 Microsoft Corporation – 1998 Edition

4. Mindscape World Atlas & Almanac – Version 6 – 1995 Mindscape, Inc.

Acknowledgements

First of all, I would like to thank God for blessing me with the opportunity to be a part of this book.

I would like to thank Cecil Rains who gave me the great honor of getting the chance to write his inspiring story. I will always be grateful for being given this opportunity.

I would like to thank Loretta Rains who cordially welcomed me into their home during the writing of this book and provided the pictures that we used for the book.

I would like to thank the distinguished veterans of World War II that I spoke with concerning the writing of this book.

I would like to thank my father, Warren G. Howard and my father in law, Durward L. Book who answered our country's call to duty to preserve our freedom.

I would like to thank my mother, Zela Ruth Howard and my mother in law, Mildred Book for their willingness to sacrifice during our country's great time of need.

I would like to thank my wife, Marla for her love and support during the many hours spent on this project.

Finally, I would like to thank Joe Glasgow and the people at Jona Books for their enthusiastic support in the publication of this book.

About the Author

T.J. Howard has been a teacher and basketball coach for several years in Southern Illinois before pursuing a writing career. His first novel, *How Far Is Heaven?* though fictional is based on some actual events in his life. He has a Bachelor's Degree in Elementary Education from Southern Illinois University and a Master's Degree and Ph.D in Biblical Studies from Louisiana Baptist University. He and his wife, Marla reside in Bonnie, Illinois.